COUNTRY CRAFTS

Anne Dyer
Lettice Sandford
Zena Edwards

Consultant: Pat Cherry
NFWI Home Economics Adviser
Weaving consultant:
Katharine Smith

BOOK CLUB ASSOCIATES
LONDON

Designed and created by
Berkeley Publishers Ltd.
9 Warwick Court
London WC1R 5DJ

Editor John Axon
Design Peter Davies
Photography Chris Ridley
Illustrations David Parr
Anne Ronan Picture Library
Pressed flower pictures kindly
lent by Evelyn Rodwell-Jones

First published 1979
Macdonald Educational Ltd.
Holywell House
Worship Street
London EC2A 2EN

This edition published 1979 by
Book Club Associates
By arrangement with
Macdonald Educational Ltd.

Editorial manager
Chester Fisher
Publishing co-ordinator
Gill Rowley
Production manager
Eva Wrennall

Made and printed by
Purnell & Sons Ltd.,
Paulton

Contents

Introduction

Every time a traditional craft is allowed to die away or is replaced by a machine process, something of value is lost from our heritage and we are left that much the poorer. Yet no one has deliberately planned this. We are victims of circumstance in this respect. Our society follows the pattern of all industrial economies, exploiting each technological advance as it arises, and in so doing the old skills—the standards of craftsmanship achieved over the centuries—have tended to be left behind.

Modern, machine-based methods of production may have their economic advantages. But what may be good for the national economy does not necessarily improve the quality of life. It is to this end that many people, both professional and amateur, have sought to revive and bring back into daily use the lost crafts and techniques of our rich rural tradition.

The National Federation of Women's Institutes has always sought to encourage traditional crafts. As Britain's biggest women's organization and one of the largest organizations of countrywomen in the world, it is in a unique position to do so. The zeal of WI members—many of whom now lecture in their chosen skills—has given a new lease of life to many traditional crafts. Craft shops today enjoy a thriving trade. They owe much of their prosperity to the craft-conscious members of the WI.

Country Crafts brings together some long-established skills. All can be quite easily mastered by following the instructions set out here by four of the WI's top craft experts. Spinning, dyeing and weaving, as well as being economically self-justifying, are among the most satisfying of all craft activities. Basketry, which must rank as one of the most ancient of all crafts, has a timeless appeal. Corn dolly-making is a skill with an ancient historical background. It is an enchanting craft to practise, with its many mythological associations and its curiously geometric designs. The materials for the art of preserving flowers are freely available in gardens, hedgerows and fields, and can be used to produce the most original and attractive collages and everlasting flower arrangements.

There is no doubt that once you have embarked upon these fascinating craft activities and discovered your own creative potential, you will never look back. A little time and patience can reward you with delightful household articles and decorative items, and the making of them will have given you hours of pleasure.

Home Economics Adviser
National Federation of Women's Institutes

Spin and weave your own fine fabrics

Spinning, weaving and dyeing are basic crafts which date back to man's earliest existence. The recent revival of interest in these ancient skills reflects not just a desire for individuality in an increasingly uniform world, but a growing appreciation of the qualities of natural materials and of the craftsmanship that can make of them something unique. Any article you have spun, woven and dyed for yourself, whether garment, tapestry or home furnishing, will carry the stamp of your own personality.

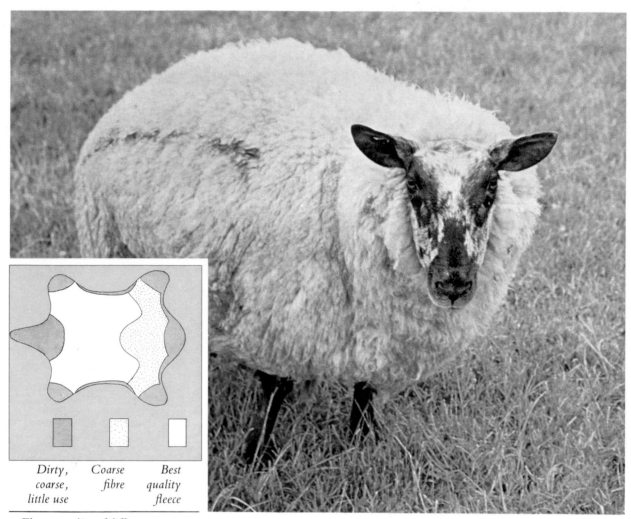

Dirty,
coarse,
little use

Coarse
fibre

Best
quality
fleece

1 *Fleece, quality of different parts*

Spinning

Early man almost certainly wove with plant fibres and hair before he discovered how to twist them together to form a continuous yarn. The art of spinning in its simplest form, with a drop spindle, can be traced back to the earliest civilizations. We also know that the one-thread wheel was in use for many centuries. Fine fabrics have been woven from flax, silk and wool for centuries and the use of vegetable dyes has helped to preserve beautiful work for many hundreds of years. As long ago as 5000 BC man had evolved fairly sophisticated weaving techniques.

Although superseded in Europe by the Saxony wheel in the fifteenth century, the drop spindle is still used in many parts of the world because of its simplicity and convenience. Beautiful tapestries, rugs, blankets and clothing are produced by many unsophisticated peoples using simple weaving equipment.

Unless you want to weave large quantities of tweed, for which in any case you would have to buy expensive yarn, elaborate and expensive looms are not essential for home weaving. It is possible to make adequate frames quite cheaply yourself on which you can weave many useful and attractive items with your own spun yarn.

Choosing a fleece

The hair or wool of almost every creature has been spun or woven at some time, but over the centuries the sheep has proved to be the most useful of beasts. It has long been domesticated, not just for its wool but also for its flesh, milk and hide. Different breeds have been evolved for different climates and terrain and selective breeding has produced various types of wool, from the toughest rug wool to the longest lustre, which can be almost like silk.

Fleece can be bought from the International Wool Secretariat, from craft suppliers or sometimes direct from the farmer. It is sold by weight, traditionally the imperial pound in the UK. The price varies from year to year and with the quality of the wool. Unless you learn to judge a fleece for yourself you are very much in the hands of the supplier and the friendly farmer may be the most helpful person to buy from.

A good fleece for general use should feel soft and greasy. Pull out a bit between your finger and thumb and see how long the staple is, that is, the length of the hair. Anything less than 10-12.5 cm (4-5 in) could be difficult to spin. Make sure the fleece is not full of little short bits or separated lumps. Also, beware of tight felted wool that will not pull apart. A really good fleece should be almost wholly spinnable, although the wool quality varies from one part of the animal to another (figure 1). In an average fleece weighing 1.75-2.25 kg (4-5 lb), you must be prepared for up to 0.5 kg (1 lb) loss of weight when it is washed and spun, depending on the amount of dirt and grease.

Some fleeces are badly felted, badly clipped or have a very short staple and can be virtually useless for spinning unless they are carded. Some cannot even be carded satisfactorily.

Fleeces vary in colour as well as quality. Many flocks are crossbred, but black sheep are usually of the Welsh mountain breed. The appearance of this breed has made it popular for domestic flocks. It is the only wholly black breed. The wool is often short and tight and not easy to spin.

Jacob sheep have become increasingly popular for small flocks and for crossing with white breeds. Crossing often produces attractive all-over grey or brown sheep. The pure Jacob should have four horns and a white fleece with brown or black spots and patches. These sheep often have very good-quality wool and are liked by spinners for the varied colours in their fleece.

Many northern breeds, Herdwick, Swaledale and Scottish, have very long stapled wool, but this is usually coarse and is most suitable for rugs. Lincolns and Leicesters, on the other hand, have very long and silky wool, which is the most expensive type. Some of the finest wool of crossbred sheep comes from the offspring of Merino ewes and English Leicester rams. The latter have heavy fleeces and the wool hangs in compact locks. They were developed in the mid-eighteenth century by Robert Bakewell.

Some fleeces are much cleaner than others, but freedom from grease is not a good quality. Mud and dirt can be a nuisance and so can a lot of grass seeds or thistles—a sudden encounter with the latter can be very painful.

It is often not realized that a coloured fleece will fade quite considerably in the summer. Many a fleece that looks brown or gingery on the sheep may prove to be mainly dark grey or black when shorn. This mixed wool spins up into an attractive yarn and is not likely to fade badly in use, unless exposed for long periods to bright sunlight.

In general, hedgerow wool and any other dead and dirty wool can be regarded as unsuitable for spinning. It is possible to spin it, but the wool is likely to be brittle and stained.

Similarly, any hair combed from dogs is also dead, smelly and inclined to be matted, though some people spin it with great success.

Sheep are dipped before shearing to help get rid of any insects in the fleece. The sheep is usually shorn in hot weather when the grease is up in the wool. Most people prefer to spin 'in the grease'—that is to say, before washing.

If the wool is washed, it is necessary to add a little oil when spinning, which seems rather a pointless practice since the natural grease is good for the hands and, in any case, it rinses off very easily.

Equipment for spinning

A drop spindle is very simple to make or can be improvised in a few minutes (figure 2). Spinning was never a specialized craft and can be quickly mastered by anyone with a little perseverance. By far the best plan is to learn to use the drop spindle before trying a wheel. Once you can manage the drop spindle you are half way there. The drop spindle can never rival the spinning

2 Improvised drop spindle, potato and skewer

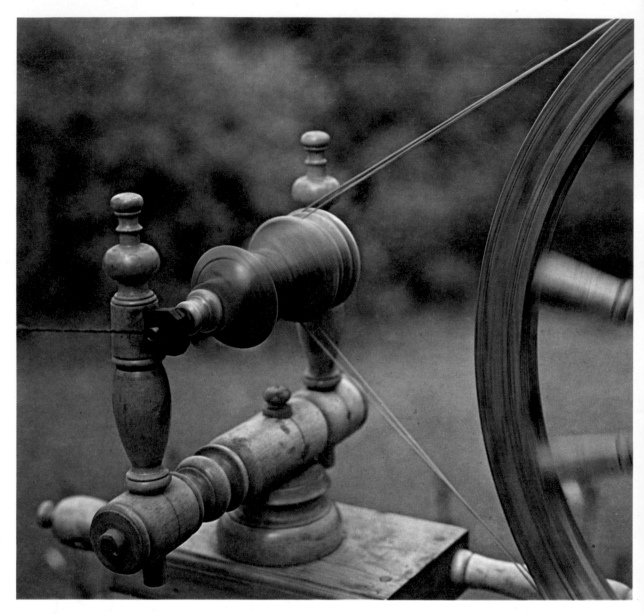

wheel for speed but, with practice, a very good thread can be spun quite quickly with this admirable piece of equipment.

The spinning wheel or Saxony wheel is the first, and possibly the only, expensive piece of equipment needed for spinning. A good deal of consideration should be given to the best type to buy. There are basically three types and provided they come from a reliable maker they will all spin equally well. It is best not to purchase an antique spinning wheel unless you have a

very good adviser. They can be expensive and quite useless for spinning; some are only built as ornaments.

Types of spinning wheel

The spinning wheel generally known as the **horizontal wheel** has the wheel alongside the spinning unit and both are mounted on a flat 'table', which may or may not be tilted at an angle. Horizontal wheels vary a great deal in size and detail and are often the largest and most expensive. They can be very

Spinning wheel in action

attractive, but unless they can be dismounted they can be very awkward to transport.

The **vertical wheel,** also of traditional design, has the spinning unit mounted above the driving wheel, which makes it more compact. It can be carried in one hand and easily laid in a car as it takes up no more than 0·5 m² (1½ ft²) of floor space. Some modern Norwegian models are very pretty and have the added advantage of built-in racks for extra bobbins. These also vary in price but they are usually in the medium range.

The **Ashford wheel** is very popular today because of its comparatively low price. It is made in kit form in New Zealand. This very functional wheel spins well, but it is rather inelegant and awkward to transport, although not as large as some horizontal wheels.

The possibility of transporting a spinning wheel may not be considered important by the beginner if space in the house is no problem. However, spinning can be one of the best of social activities.

Additional implements
Carders (figure 3) are useful tools, but are not essential to begin with. It is a waste of time to card a good fleece. It is just as easy, or easier, to spin direct from the fleece and there will be no difference in the resulting quality of yarn.

Having spun most of your fleece, there will come a time when you will be left with a quantity of poor-quality wool—there is some in every fleece. Unless you are prepared to tease every scrap by hand, you must card the remainder to spin it or you could wash the wool and use it for stuffing toys or cushions.

Carders are expensive to buy but they are simple to make if you buy the spiney card cloths from a craft supplier. These can cost as little as £2 a pair, certainly less than half the price of the complete article. The wooden base can be cut from a piece of good quality deal 1·90 cm (¾ in) thick or 1·25 cm (½ in) ply. Cut the handle in one piece with the grain going the length of the handle. Card cloths are usually about 12·5 x 20 cm (5 x 8 in) and the wood should be cut 2·5 cm (1 in) larger. Rub down thoroughly, rounding the handles, and nail the cloths on round the edges with carpet or tin tacks, not more than 2·5 cm (1 in) apart. A punch is a help when knocking them in. Be sure to get the spines of the cards leaning towards the handles. Bought carders sometimes have curved backs but this is no advantage.

When you wind the wool off your spindle or bobbin you will need a holder for it. You can use a box with a hole in each side through which you poke each end of the drop spindle (figure 4). Or when using a bobbin, stick a knitting needle through it. Later, a rack or **lazy kate** can be very simply made.

To wind the yarn into a hank, the legs of an upturned chair are quite handy but a **niddy noddy** is simple to make with a length of broomstick about 0·5 m (21 in) long and two lengths of dowelling about the size of a pencil 17·5 cm (7 in) long (figure 5). Bore a hole 7·5 cm (3 in) from each end of the broomstick to take the two lengths of dowelling firmly and at right angles to each other.

Now you have all you need to begin spinning.

How to use a drop spindle

The drop spindle consists of a round wooden whorl like the head of a mushroom with a 30-cm (1-ft) length of dowelling pushed through a hole in the middle. You can cut a notch like a crotchet hook in the top end of the dowelling, but this is not essential. The whorl should be made to fit firmly one-third of the length from the bottom end. Or you can easily improvise one with a skewer stuck through a small potato (as in figure 2). The question of weight and balance is a matter of experience, but it can be made to work very well.

Take about 1 m (3 ft) of ready-spun wool and tie one end to the

4 Improvised lazy kate, shoe box

3 Carders

spindle just above the whorl. Take the wool down over the whorl, round the spindle below it and up to the top where you make a half hitch over the hook or tip of the spindle. Tie a small loop in the end of the wool.

Take a handful of fleece in the left hand, pull out some fibres with the right hand and double it through the loop in the wool on the spindle. Give the spindle a sharp twist and let it drop. While it twists, pull out some more fleece with the right hand and slide the right finger and thumb up to the left with the twist and with the left finger and thumb stop the twist running into the rest of the fleece.

Give the spindle repeated twists to keep it going. Do not let it unwind or the thread will break. Repeat until the spindle is touching the ground—you can spin a greater length at a time if you stand up to do it. Now wind the wool you have spun on to the spindle above the whorl, leaving enough to take down over the whorl, round the bottom and up to the top. Again, slip the half hitch over the tip and continue until the spindle is getting full. When it is full it gets heavy and the yarn may break. If the yarn breaks, tease out the end and lay it in the fleece. When the twist runs up it will draw the fibres out with it.

Do not worry if the yarn is rough and lumpy. Once you have mastered the knack of keeping it going without breaking, you will be able to make a better thread by regulating the amount that you pull out of the fleece. The better you can spin with a drop spindle, the easier you will find it to use a spinning wheel.

When the spindle is full enough, wind the yarn off into a hank on the niddy noddy. You can stop the spindle from rolling around by poking the ends through the sides of a shoe box. To use a niddy noddy (see figure 5), hold it by the bottom

in your right hand, together with the end of the yarn. With the left hand pull the yarn from the bobbin or spindle and take it up over arm A from right to left, down round arm B, right to left, up and over arm C from right to left and down round arm D from right to left, which brings you back where you started. Continue following the first round exactly, always going right to left and taking care never to cross over. Take the yarn round loosely, never at all tightly or the arms may break. Tie the two ends

Three types of spinning wheel

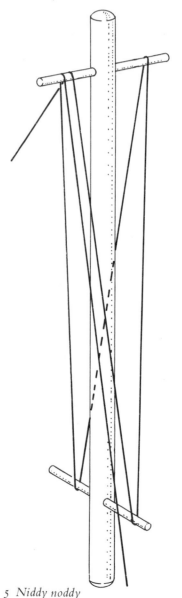

5 *Niddy noddy*

together firmly and, following carefully round the hank while it is still on the niddy noddy, tie it round firmly but loosely in at least four places with a spare piece of wool. Slip the hank off the arms; it is now ready for washing.

How to use a spinning wheel

The spinning wheel is the most complicated piece of equipment you are likely to need. On most spinning wheels the driving belt goes twice round the driving wheel, once round the drive spool which turns the spindle and fliers and once round the spool on the bobbin which revolves on the spindle. In this way the wool is simultaneously twisted into yarn and wound upon the bobbin (figure 6). On the Ashford wheel, however, there is only the single belt driving the flier, with a separate tensioner to brake the spool.

You will have to do two things at once—work the treadle which turns the wheel and the whole spinning unit, and feed the wool evenly and rhythmically into the hole at the end of the spindle.

Make sure you are sitting comfortably, not too low, and practise treadling the wheel. Make it go clockwise, then change to anti-clockwise. Learn to stop and start without using your hand. Treadle as slowly as you can without checking.

Now tie one end of a 90-cm (3-ft)

length of spun wool firmly round the bobbin and fix it in place with a bit of sticky tape to stop it from slipping. Slipping may be the cause of a mysterious failure to wind on. Lead the wool over a central hook on one of the fliers and take it through the nearest hole in the side of the spindle and out at the end facing you. A piece of fine but firm wire (a hairpin, for instance) with a tiny hook at the end is used to draw the wool through. You will need this often, so tie a bit of line to a loop in the other end of the wire and anchor it safely to the spinning wheel.

Tie a loop in the end of wool that you have drawn through and adjust the tension of the driving belt fairly loosely. The method of adjusting tension varies from one wheel to another, but can be easily identified. Take a handful of fleece in your left hand, draw some out and as when using the drop spindle, double it

6 *Spinning wheel*

through the loop in the wool. Start to treadle gently, turning the wheel clockwise. The wool will be twisted and drawn into the hole in the spindle. Let it run in but do not let the twist run up into the fleece. You

Weighing weld for dyeing

7 *Drying hanks*

now have two hands with which to control it. Let your right finger and thumb slide up with the twist towards the left and pull out more fleece. In time you will find your own rhythm.

If the yarn seems to be drawn in too fast, slacken the tension. If it is twisting up too tightly and not running in enough, tighten the tension—but check that you are not holding on to the wool too tightly. A very slight adjustment in the tension makes a difference. As before, do not worry about the lumpy bits. Select the best parts of fleece to use until you have got the hang of it. Shift the yarn on to different hooks on the fliers so that it winds up evenly on to the bobbin. As the bobbin fills you will find that you need to tighten the tension slightly.

When the bobbin is full you can

either wind it into a hank as it is, or spin a second bobbinful and ply the two together. To wind it off on the niddy noddy, slacken the main tension and slip the belt off the bobbin spool, which will then turn freely. It is generally better to ply wool needed for knitting unless it is spun very softly since it tends to twist the fabric. It is not necessary to ply yarn for weaving unless needed for extra strength for warp. Thicker yarn is made by spinning it thicker in the first instance, not by plying more together. When two bobbins are full of yarn put them on a lazy kate, double the two ends through the loop of wool on another bobbin and spin them together in an anticlockwise direction. You need to have at least three bobbins.

Washing the yarn

Even if the wool looks clean, begin by rinsing the hanks thoroughly in a bucket of cool clear water. You will be surprised at the resulting strong tea-like brew, which, incidentally, is good liquid manure for the garden. Never waste soap on this first rinse. Fine soft wool is then best washed in not too hot water and soap flakes. If your water is hard you will need some water softener or no lather will be produced. Detergent is perfectly satisfactory for the coarse wool used for rugs and tapestries. In any case, rinse until the water is clear. Then squeeze out the yarn or spin dry and hang up to dry under slight tension—particularly if it is not plied (figure 7). When spin-drying, tie the hanks in a firm bundle or roll them up in a bag to prevent tangling.

Carding

Carders consist of a pair of identical boards measuring about 24 x 12·5 cm (9½ x 5 in) each with a handle on the longest side (see figure 3). The front of each of the carders

is covered with fine wire hooks.

To card, take a carder in your left hand and rest it on your knee with the handle to the left. Spread a small bit of fleece on the hooks and gently pull the right-hand carder across from left to right combing the fleece out several times until it it smooth and tidy.

Then turn the carders so that they are face to face with the handles on the same side and firmly push the right-hand carder across the left-hand one from left to right—until the wool is all on the left carder again.

Turn both carders to the original position but *push* the right-hand carder across the left from right to left, and the wool should form a a sausage or 'rolag' which can be detached and laid by ready for spinning. This is usually sufficient though can be repeated if it is still a bit rough.

If you have to card, it is probably best to do it in the garden as carding tends to be a messy business. Carding will make it possible to spin almost any sort of fleece somehow— even if only suitable for rugs. Fairly rough fleece can be used in tapestries to give added texture. However, no amount of carding will enable you to spin really good yarn from bad fleece. You cannot expect to spin gold from straw.

In the summer, when you can work in the garden, it is a good idea to rough-card all the poor-quality residue in the bottom of your wool sacks and spin it into more-or-less rope for rug-making. The dirtiest bits can be dipped in a bucket of water and then spread on wire netting to dry in the sun before carding. This minimal wash does not destroy the oil.

Fleeces can be put into large polythene bags and labelled with such details as the type and colour of fleece, the supplier and the date. The fleece can be spun straight from the bag, selecting the better pieces to spin until there are none left. When you have bought many

Dyeing at home

different-coloured fleeces, you may spin only a little from one bag at a time. Fleeces can be kept in perfect condition if stored in this way. They do not seem to attract moths if left unwashed but they may become dry if they are stored for too long.

Dyeing

Vegetable dyes

Even if coloured fleeces are available, it is worthwhile exploring the wealth of vegetable dyes to hand in the countryside. They are not easier or more reliable than chemical dyes but they give a quality of colour which is difficult to equal in commercially dyed wool. This may be partly due to the lustre and texture of handspun wool and a slight unevenness of colour which might be considered a fault but in fact adds greatly to the quality. Vegetable dyes used on machine-spun wool can be disappointing to use because of the resulting evenness of texture and colour.

Vegetable dyes are not difficult to use, and they are very rewarding. The only essentials are a fairly large saucepan which should be reserved for the purpose, and of course a source of heat. A special dye-room is not needed. If the kitchen cannot be used, you can manage with some sort of cooker such as a Primus or gas ring if there is water laid on nearby. If using the kitchen, some of the smellier dye-plants are better avoided at meal-times.

Old enamel pans are quite adequate for dyeing, and a lid is an asset. Large pans are expensive to buy new, but old pans can be used satisfactorily.

A big pan should take over 225 g (8 oz) of yarn, but you seldom dye so much at a time. Some dyes stain the pans quite badly but they can

always be scoured after use. An old wooden spoon can be used for dyeing, and it is a good idea to attach a piece of string to stop it from falling into the dye pan.

In general, too much emphasis is placed on cleanliness, and would-be dyers tend to be put off by the do's and don'ts. However, when using chemicals for mordants, keep everything well away from children. Few of the chemicals are lethal, but if, for instance, a child were to investigate a bag of powdered indigo, he would take a good deal of cleaning up.

Mordanting

Before using most dyes, yarn must be simmered with one of four or five chemicals called mordants. Neglecting this may cause disappointment. The most useful chemicals are alum, chrome, iron, tin and cream of tartar.

Alum (potassium aluminium sulphate) and cream of tartar are the only mordants that can now be bought from a chemist. They are non-poisonous and generally useful for the beginner.

Other mordants can be bought in small quantities from craft suppliers, and, more cheaply, in large quantities from educational suppliers. Different mordants give different results with the same plant.

Chrome, or potassium dichromate, gives more golden or mustard yellows, generally duller than alum.

Iron (ferrous sulphate) which must be used with cream of tartar, gives lovely sludgy greens, browns and greys.

Tin or stannous chloride, also with cream of tartar, gives the brightest orange and reddish colours.

To mordant 225 g (8 oz) wool you will need:
Alum: 40-55 g (1½-2 oz)
plus 12 g (½ oz) cream of tartar
(The larger quantity is for coarse wool.)
Chrome: 7 g (¼ oz)
Tin: 7 g (¼ oz)

plus 25 g (1 oz) cream of tartar
Iron: 7 g (¼ oz)
plus 25 g (1 oz) cream of tartar

The procedure can be the same in all cases but iron and tin are sometimes added to the dye pot.

Dissolve thoroughly in a pan with enough water to cover the yarn completely. While heating, add 225 g (8 oz) yarn, thoroughly wetted and with a string passed through the hanks and loosely knotted. The string is useful for enabling you to lift and move the yarn so that you can inspect it for colour. Bring to the boil and simmer for 45 minutes, keeping the end of the string out of the pan. The wool is now mordanted and can be dyed now or later. There is no need to rinse but it must be wetted before dyeing.

Weld in the garden

Dyeing yellows and oranges

Reseda luteola or weld is worth a special mention as it is one of the oldest and best dye plants. A biennial, once cultivated for the purpose it grows almost too easily in the garden, though possibly not in acid soils. It can be found growing in poor soil on derelict land or by the roadside. In good soil it will grow to over 2 m (6 ft) high. You do not need the root and if you cut the top instead of pulling the plant up it will make new growth the same year. Weld smells strongly of horseradish when you gather it but far worse when cooking it green. It gives the same excellent dye at any stage of growth up to November. It can be dried, chopped and stored for years in a sack.

Weld gives the purest yellow

with an alum mordant and is also valuable combined with blues to give bright greens. Seed can be bought from craft suppliers. It is slow to germinate but you will have it for ever, if you let it seed.

Other plants which give good yellows are goldenrod, ragwort, and tansy.

Dyeing bright yellow

To dye bright yellow you will need:
100 g (4 oz) wool mordanted with alum and cream of tartar
225 g (8 oz) chopped green weld or other plant or 100 g (4 oz) dry plant material

These quantities are right for most plants, allowing a double quantity if the plant is fresh.

Put the plant in a pan of water and

bring slowly to the boil. Add the wool while heating, or wait until the colour has been extracted and remove some of the dye plant to make more room for the wool. Simmer for 20 minutes. Lift the yarn to inspect the colour.

It if is weak, you may need more plant material—lack of sun makes a difference. If the water has completely lost its colour, the wool has taken up all the colour there was. You can simmer for longer but the colour is unlikely to deepen after 30 minutes. Take the yarn out and shake it well to remove bits, rinse until the water is clear.

Dyeing brilliant orange

Keep a cardboard box by the sink for saving the brown outer skins of onions. Have a good panful—they are impossible to weigh. Press them down in the water with the wetted wool. There is no smell now or later. Bring slowly to boil and simmer. Lift out the wool and add the tin and cream of tartar well dissolved in a jar of water and stir well before returning the wool to the pan. Simmer until bright enough and finish as before.

Dyeing other colours

Onion skins dye a wonderful burnt orange on wool mordanted with chrome or a golden yellow mordanted with alum and cream of tartar. Iron mordant will give a dark brown. Onion skins are worth saving and the dye is fairly fast and varies very little.

The mature outer leaves of red cabbage dye a pretty slatey blue with any mordant, but tin is best.

Dyeing with woad

Woad is easily grown from seed and everyone knows that the ancient Britons scared the Romans by dyeing their bodies blue with it. It was extensively cultivated in

East Anglia up to the end of the last century and is worth growing in the garden for the sake of its showers of tiny brilliant yellow flowers and later the rows of hanging black pods. The flowers dye a good yellow but to get blue is not so simple and can be very smelly.

Woad grows wild in the Middle East and it is now believed the dye may have originated there. Its use dates back to very early times, but it was only introduced into Britain shortly before Caesar landed. The woad plant is known botanically as *Isatis tinctoria*.

Dyeing with madder

You can grow madder in the garden, and its roots dye the loveliest rosy red. However, you may have to wait several years before you can dig enough for dyeing. Craft suppliers sell madder root in powdered form. Madder floats on the surface of the water, so mix it to a paste with water and a little cream of tartar before adding to the dyebath.

To dye 225 g (8 oz) wool mordanted with alum and cream of tartar use 50 g (2 oz) madder mixed up with 25 g (1 oz) tartar. Bring it very slowly to the boil. Add a little cold water and the wetted wool. Keep it just under simmering point for 45 minutes. If you boil it fast it will dye a tan colour, but to obtain a true rose red very gentle heat is needed.

Dyeing with logwood chips

Logwood dyes dull grey-blue with a chrome mordant and purple with alum but its greatest use is with weld to give good soft greens. Use a chrome mordant for green.

A pinch of logwood can be used to tone down a harsh indigo blue. However, it is very strong and it is all too easy to end up with an almost black yarn by mistake. Domestic bleach has no effect on it but Dygon shifts it slightly with some interest-

ing, if unpremeditated, results. Always use much less logwood than you think you need. You can add more but not subtract. Try 5 ml (1 teaspoon) to 225 g (8 oz) wool.

Dyeing with cochineal

Cochineal (the insects, not the bottled essence) is very expensive now. Used alone, it dyes a hideous crimson, but when combined with weld it produces a good red, and is fine with logwood or indigo for producing purples.

Dyeing with indigo

Indigo dyes the bluest of all blues and, along with weld and madder, is one of the oldest dyes. Indigo comes as a very fine blue powder which has a tendency to seep through even several layers of polythene. It is insoluble in water so experts use the indigo vat system, which seems rather a lot of trouble to take unless a large quantity of yarn is to be dyed. It is perfectly satisfactory, however, to make extract of indigo stock solution. The only problem is in obtaining sulphuric acid. This is both dangerous and expensive. However, a little goes a long way. Do use rubber gloves.

You need a 1-kg (2-lb) jam jar, a glass rod for stirring and a half-litre (1 pint) bottle with a glass stopper for storing.

225 g (8 oz) sulphuric acid
25 g (1 oz) powdered indigo
12 g (½ oz) precipitated chalk

Put the indigo into the jar, pour a little acid on to it and mix with a glass rod. It will effervesce and get quite hot. Add a little chalk. Stir well and add a little more acid and so on until all is used up. Go gently or it may effervesce over the top. Store in the stoppered jar. Stir it now and then and add a little more chalk. It will be fit to use after a week.

This quantity will dye a lot of wool. The extract is very strong and needs no mordant. You must how-ever use an alum mordant if you plan to overdye for green or purple. Simply pour about 5 ml (1 teaspoon) of extract into the dye pot, stir well and add the wetted wool. Bring to simmering point and the wool will quickly take up the dye. If not deep enough, lift out the wool and stir in more indigo. Simmer for 30 minutes and, if there is still colour in the water, you can go on adding hank after hank of yarn getting paler and paler blues—all of them beautiful—until the water is clear and the pan unstained. Light shades can always be overdyed with weld or cochineal and the results can be exciting. Separate strands of plied yarn may not take the dye equally. Colour changes are end-lessly fascinating.

Other vegetable dyes

Any plant is worth a try, but you are unlikely to derive much satis-faction by experimenting with sea-weed or fungi. Never use plants that are at all rare. Common weeds give good colours. In fact, almost every plant yields some colour.

Lichens are another story. They are abundant in certain places but take many years to grow. Although much used for dyeing in the past, their use today is not encouraged because, as the numbers of dyeing enthusiasts increase, the plants could eventually disappear completely.

Other dyestuffs

Craft suppliers offer various other dyestuffs, but experience has shown that sufficient colours can be obtained from the materials men-tioned. Many subtle colours, ideal for tapestries, can be obtained from wild plants. If your first attempt with a dyestuff produces a useless colour, dip the yarn into something else. This will often produce some-thing interesting. Wash the yarns thoroughly to make sure the colours will not run and leave them out in

the sun to see if they will fade. If they do, overdye them. Do not use soap. Clean water is enough.

Once you have developed an interest in dyeing, a bundle of yarns will often inspire the ultimate use. But, whether muted or bril-liant, there is a use for almost any colour or tone—and certainly any-thing you have dyed yourself will have a character as individual as an artist's palette, never to be repeated or copied.

If you should think of using vegetable dyes on bought wool, be careful that it is pure wool and has not been treated against moth or staining. This may make it dye-proof. Synthetics tend to be very uncertain. Some cheap yarn is vir-tually impossible to dye.

Test dyeing

Anne Dyer, in her book *Dyes from Natural Sources*, writes of her method of test-dyeing in a small vacuum flask. Such a flask should be kept specially for test-dyeing and not used for any other purpose.

Mordant four hanks of wool with alum, chrome, iron and tin respec-

8 Knots for test dyeing

tively, and mark the ends of each hank in alphabetical order with one, two, three or four overhand knots (figure 8). Cut 15 cm (6 in) off the end of each hank, including knots—and before you forget, knot the cut ends. Put the four lengths

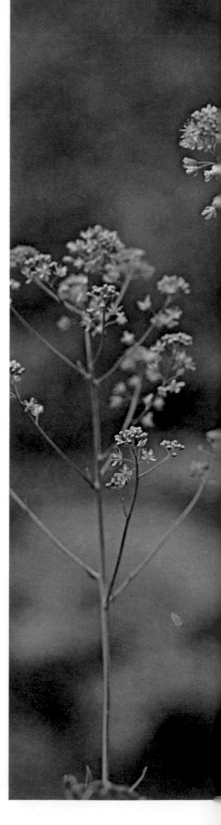

Woad brightening up the garden

into the vacuum flask with scraps of whatever plant you have brought in from the garden and fill up with boiling water. Screw down and leave it for an hour or more. You will probably find four different-coloured bits of wool. Often they will run in the green-to-yellow range, often they will be very dull. With some plants—St John's wort, red-seeding heads of dock, foxglove—you will get pinky golds and orange, and with prunus leaves a good green. You may find something really exciting.

Keep a record of what, where and when you dyed. Although these dyes are variable and unreliable, you will have at least a rough guide for reference and the knots will show which mordant was used. A few drops of ammonia or vinegar may produce a change of colour.

Weaving

Weaving on simple frames

Weaving is not difficult. To weave, a warp is needed together with some means of keeping it taut, and a weft which is woven in and out of the warp threads. These can be lifted mechanically on a loom which has pedals or levers which open the sheds through which the weft is passed. On a simple frame, one set of warp threads is lifted with a shed stick. For the return trip, the weft must be woven in and out by hand. This may at first seem tedious and it is possible to rig leashes to lift the other warps. This extra complication is not really worth the trouble, particularly for tapestry weaving.

It is said that a weaver with a foot loom needs six to eight spinners in order to be kept supplied with yarn. This type of loom can produce materials and rugs fairly quickly,

Vegetable dyed hanks over weaving frame

though not of course as quickly as they can be woven in a factory. Weaving like this is a mechanical process. The loom is set up. The weaver works the pedals and throws the shuttle to and fro with the weft. A steady rhythm achieves an even result which is almost comparable to the commercial article.

A foot loom is expensive to buy even secondhand and takes up a lot of room. Putting on a warp is a long job and difficult to do single-handed.

With a few ordinary tools and pieces of timber you can make frames on which exciting things can be woven at home.

For weaving small samplers on your lap you need:
a firm plywood board about 25 x 37·5 cm (10 x 15 in)
3 pieces of clean wood about 3·75 x 1·87 cm (1½ x ¾ in) and 25 cm (10 in) long
a thin piece of plywood about 2·5 x 25 cm (1 x 10 in)—a ruler will do
100 g (4 oz) panel pins 165 mm (⅝ in) long—not smaller. These will be enough for a larger frame too. They are small, almost headless, nails. Avoid tin-tacks or anything similar.

Sizes suggested here are approximate but frames should always be at least half as long again as they are wide. Smooth all wood down thoroughly.

Glue and nail one of the 25-cm (10-in) lengths to each end of the board (figure 9). Starting 1·25 cm

9 *Small frame*

(½ in) from the left-hand top corner A and 1·25 cm (½ in) down mark with a small bradawl a row of holes 1·25 cm (½ in) apart. The nails must all lean slightly outwards and it helps if the holes are correctly raked first. Make an identical row of holes 1·25 cm (½ in) below and in between the first holes (figure 10). Knock the nails in accurately leaving 60 mm (¼ in) sticking out. Starting from the bottom left-hand corner B put in two more similar rows starting 1·25 cm (½ in) from side and bottom edges at B and sloping outwards.

This little frame is ideal for trying out techniques, colour combinations and new ideas. It can be used to make a tiny tapestry or mat and is a nice present for a child to begin on. You will need thin string, a large tapestry or packing needle and a kitchen fork. To warp up (figure 11), tie a slip knot in the end of the string and tighten it over the

10 *Nails in frame, note angle*

11 *Warping up, knots (A) slip (B) clove*

19

Using the weaving hook

first nail at A. Take it down round the first nail at B and also round the nearest diagonal one. Up and round the next nail at the top and the nearest diagonal and so on to the end. Keep the string taut but not strained. Finish off with several firm half hitches round the last nail.

Weave the thin strip of wood over and under alternate warp threads, push it to the top and leave it there. This is your shed stick (figure 12). The other length of

12 Shed stick and tension stick

wood goes under the whole warp, turned on its side and pushed down to the bottom. It keeps the warp taut and the weaving clear of the nails (figure 12). This arrangement of nails allows you to warp up with four, eight, ten or twelve ends to the inch according to what you want to do. Four to the inch is enough to begin with (figure 13).

Wool for the weft can be wound on to a card or bobbin, or wound into a butterfly (figure 14). These methods are rather unhandy compared with a weaving hook made

20

from a slip of straight-grained wood about 60 mm ($\frac{1}{4}$ in) thick or less and about 1·90 cm ($\frac{3}{4}$ in) wide (figure 15). Pare down and taper the sides and ends with a sharp knife and cut hooks on opposite sides. Rub down very thoroughly. If a hook breaks it is easily re-cut and rubbed down. You cannot buy these, but it will be worth your while to make one yourself. You simply wiggle the hook in and out and pull the wool through—often 2-3 m (2-3 yd) of yarn. It is far quicker than threading a needle for each change of colour. Bobbins have to be secured every time and can only be poked through a few warp ends at a time. The hook will draw through as far as it will reach.

When pulling the weft through from right to left hold the right-hand selvedge firmly to prevent the weft being pulled up too tightly and do the same when working the other way. Always keep the weft slack or the work will get out of shape. When starting to weave turn the shed stick on edge to open the shed and pull a length of warp right through leaving about 2·5 cm (1 in) hanging out. Turn the shed stick flat and tuck the end in between the other warps. Wiggle the weft back again and over the tucked-in tail.

When using the hook you will find you can slip it easily through the stick shed without actually bothering to turn the stick. This you cannot do if using a bobbin or

butterfly. Repeat and keep the weft loose and push it well down on to the tension stick with the fork. Measure the width constantly and correct it if it is getting too tight. It takes quite a lot of practice to keep the edges straight. The weft must completely cover the string. Quite a number of rows is needed to produce an inch of tapestry well beaten down. Kelim rugs are woven in the same way. When weaving materials using similar yarns for warp and weft, both are visible. In tapestry-weaving a new piece of yarn is introduced by overlapping for 5-7·5 cm (2-3 in). Loose ends are left at the back and beaten down firmly. The needle is handy for the little frame but the hook is far quicker.

Weaving a sampler

To start your sampler (figure 16), weave about 2·5 cm (1 in) of your chosen colour and then try introducing a second colour. Work alternate rows of, say, brown and grey. When changing colour at the edge cross the yarns over each other to prevent the last warp pulling back through the same shed. Work about six rows in this way so you have a row of surprising vertical lines. Now repeat the last colour and then alternate for six more rows and you will have chequers. Now build up a mountain on the left side. Take brown wool about half way across from the left and take it back.

Repeat, but every other row turn back two warps short from the time before. Notice the angle. Slope off more obliquely by turning sooner until it ends at the edge.

With blue wool fill up the other side of your frame right up to the brown. This is the lake. Run in some thin pieces of white yarn with the blue here and there. Let them cross over and not lie side by side, to give a more watery effect, suggesting reflections. When the lake is half way up the mountain put in another hill on the right-hand side. Use a distant grey or green. Put some more white into the water and, if there is room, a paler mountain in the distance. Gradually blend water into sky by using more white and less blue. Beat down well all the time.

The first mountain will have sloped off the edge. Take some sky over the middle one and then over

15 *Weaving hook*

13 *Alternative warping*

14 *Cards or butterflies*

16 *Sampler, order of weaving*

the most distant mountain. Streak lines of grey or blue across the sky but keep it on the pale side. How about a big red sun? It is good practice and not difficult to weave a circle. Cut a round of paper about 5 cm (2 in) in diameter and fix it in position with a clothes peg behind the warp. Fill in the lower part of the sky behind the sun following the shape of the paper pattern on both sides. Using the needle and red wool fill in the sun. The sides will have to be vertical for about 2·5 cm (1 in) or you will end up with an egg in the sky.

A slit between sun and sky is quite permissible but a streak of dark cloud will look dramatic running right across both sky and sun and will hold the slit together. Beat down watching the sun shape and check your edges all the time. Fill in the sky behind the upper part of the sun and then try some lozenge-shaped clouds. Build up a wide diamond shape in grey. Start on three warps, then increase each end and every other row until about 5 cm (2 in) wide and then decrease in the same way. Beat it down and then take the white weft right over the whole thing and back again. Do several rows like this. It is very effective. You can fill in the hollows with more lozenges in grey and swoop the white over the whole.

At the top of the frame the warp gets tight and is harder to weave. Keep the weft very loose and fill in back and forth to get it level. Finish with two or three wefts worked right across and beat down. With needle and thread roughly over-sew top and bottom edges to stop unravelling.

Cut the warp close to the nails and tie overhand knots in pairs or fours close to the weaving (figure 17). Remove cotton oversewing. If the warp ends are too short to knot fold them under and stitch. To hang up your sampler, turn in a hem or stitch on a sleeve at the

17 Knotting warp ends

top to take a piece of bamboo. The tails at the back can be trimmed but left at least 2·5 cm (1 in) long for tapestry. Rugs, on the other hand, should be reversible with no tails left.

Larger frames

A larger frame is useful for shoulder bags and cushions. It will need to be rested on a table or better still hung from a hook for working but is otherwise just the same as the first frame. You need straight, clean timber about 5 x 2·5 cm (2 x 1 in). Cut three pieces 50 cm (20 in) long and two pieces for the sides about 75 cm (30 in) long. Anything larger would be rather awkward to use. Fix it firmly together (figure 18) with two screws per corner, one from the back and one from the front. Right angles are essential. Do not halve the joints. You do not want it all on the same plane like a

18 Larger frame

19 Joining warp, sheet bend

picture frame. Panel pins are put in exactly as for the little frame. The third 50-cm (20-in) length is for your tension stick and you will need a longer shed stick. Buy some thin flax, cotton or hemp line for warp. If you have to join when warping up, use a nail and sheet bend, not a reef knot (figure 19).

Techniques

Tapestry weavers often advise working from the back and pulling the loose ends tight towards you. There are no advantages and many disadvantages in this. The worst thing is that you cannot see your work and are forced to use a cartoon fixed behind the warp. This destroys all freedom of working and turns out like an exercise in painting by numbers. It also makes it impossible to introduce three-dimensional effects or textures with any confidence. Short ends can be threaded on the needle and pushed through head first to the back when working from the front. It is essential to be able to stand away and look at your work.

When weaving, it is much easier to work a horizontal line than a vertical. Subjects such as trees and buildings therefore lend themselves to sideways working—but then buildings have horizontals as well. It may be necessary to work a tapestry sideways if it is to be much wider than it is tall. In a large tapestry the weight of the woollen weft can compress badly if it is hung by the warp but for anything measuring less than one metre (one yard) this is not important. One must be guided by the subject and it is not as difficult as might be imagined to get the knack of seeing sideways.

Weaving trees and buildings can be done vertically by splitting the warps (figure 20).

Warp up the frame using eight warps every 2·5 cm (1 in). Begin by treating two warps as one. Weave a band in dark wool about 2·5 cm (1 in) deep over two and under two. Now select about a dozen pairs of warp ends 5 cm (2 in) from the left edge. With the tip of the weaving hook separate each pair leaving one from each behind the hook. Slip in a strip of card or thin wood.

Weave right across the tapestry in the usual way but go in and out of the warps behind the card only. Use a light green yarn. Work about 2·5 cm (1 in) deep.

With a dark wool weave the warps that are left in front in two separate bands to suggest two trees in the foreground. Gradually draw the weft rather tight to show the light colour between the trees. Occasionally take the weft right through the background with a needle and back again to hold it all in place. After about 2·5 cm (1 in) separate the warps on one side in the same way. Work the background right across in a bright sunny yellow. Instead of weaving

An assortment of woven articles, rug, cushion cover, tabard, bag and hassock

these front warps, wrap the dark weft round them in pairs or threes using a needle; in this way you produce thinner trees. Tuck the ends firmly through the background. You will now have sunshine showing through the trees. The larger trees can be diminished or branched as the tapestry proceeds. The branches can ultimately be returned to the original warp positions with foliage of chunky Turkey knotting. You will no doubt want to work out your own ideas at this stage.

Warp splitting is useful for buildings as they can be made to overlap. The furthest building must be worked first and needs only to be taken two or three warps behind its neighbour. Catch them together now and then. Large windows can be recessed and fantastic slits and slots woven. Wrapped warps can be divided and joined again like wire netting. You must use your ingenuity and imagination.

The normal way to work a vertical colour change is either by interlacing or leaving a slit. The latter can be sewn up afterwards or left open. To interlace, simply take the two colours on alternate rows round a central warp. This makes a finely toothed join which is of no consequence in fine wool but unsightly in thick. Another way is to weave straight up one side and join the other colour in with a needle every few rows as you work up.

A needle can also be used when building up a complicated shape with overhangs. It is tiresome to work this right across row by row and very tedious to undo if it looks wrong. The shape can be built up alone on the warp and adjusted up or down for position allowing complete freedom of design. It must be thoroughly compressed as it is worked, or your elephant may end up the wrong shape.

20 *Double weaving*

There are other ideas which add interest and emphasis. Sumak (figure 21) is useful for lines or blocks of texture, as it makes a good ridge. Turkey knots (figure 22) can be trimmed to short fur or left shaggy or even as loops.

Some people add rough embroidery after the tapestry is completed. Faces of small-scale people can be helped with a stitch or two, but it is possible to get many effects with the weaving.

Designing

Do not worry too much about design. Build up shapes, try out different colours and see what comes. Let the colour and texture guide you. Newspaper photos and monochrome prints of paintings can be useful. Anything with fairly broad blocks of different tones is best. Avoid any very detailed work. Faithful copying, particularly of colour, is impossible. A full-scale drawing tends to reduce the craft to mere copying. Keep your sketch beside you by all means and plot the salient points and angles by marking the warp with a felt pen, but do not worry if the tapestry comes out different. You will have put something of yourself into it. Walk away and look at it from the other side of the room. You will be surprised to see how much better it looks. Break up the colours. Short pieces of single yarn in assorted colours are useful to run in with the main colour and can alter the tone considerably. A streak of yellow will put sunshine on the grass. A brown or blue thread will make shadows. Do not be afraid to swoop the weft up and down over hummocks: it can be very effective, but watch tension and edges. Fill in hollows by running to and fro and level it all up when you get near the top. Keep measuring carefully and do not get careless in your haste to finish. If you can bear to leave the tapestry on the frame for a day or two after you have finished weaving, push the shed stick well down on the weaving and the yarn will crimp to the shape of the warp and pull in less when tension is released. Oversew as before. When the tapestry is off the frame, always knot the warp. If it is long, a little simple plaiting gives a good finish, but too much macramé and fancy knotting will detract from the weaving. Fix it on a strong stretcher which will not bend.

Weaving a bag

A wool warp is more difficult to use as it is more elastic, but this middle-sized frame is ideal for shoulder bags and cushion covers. Use a plied-wool warp put on tightly. If the wool is thick, four warps 2·5 cm (1 in) is enough. Experiment with colours using wide blocks of different bright colours for the warp. Run broad bands of the same colours across for the weft and see how the colours change. You will find that vegetable-dyed colours seldom conflict. The weft now must not be beaten down over the warp but should be spaced equally, four rows to 2·5 cm (1 in) if that is the warp spacing. However, if the weft is thinner than the warp you will need to beat it closer. As there is so much to learn about colour, you will want to experiment for yourself. Some colours woven across each other disappear while others are intensified. Your efforts are unlikely to be too ugly to turn into shoulder bags. natural fleece colours are always attractive.

You can work out bands of little patterns on squared paper and try skipping the weft over three warps at regular intervals. Stagger them for herringbone or chevrons. It is interesting to try, but looks rather like the machine-made folkweave or foot-loom weaving. It is better to use your greater freedom with the frame on which anything can be done. For bags you can build up shapes and work blocks or rows of contrasting Sumak or turkey knotting. You can introduce colour changes whenever you like. But beware of stripes and tartans: they can be very tedious.

Use your experiments for a bag. If the frame is long enough, it can be woven in one length and then folded. Usually a bag is woven in

21 Sumak

22 Turkey knots

23 Plaits

two pieces as it needs to be longer than it is broad. Many people like a fringe.

Oversew before cutting off. Stitch the sides together inside out. Turn and push the fringes out and knot them together at the bottom. The bag should be lined with strong material of a congenial colour. If the bag is unlined, the bottom must be stitched as well as knotted. Turn the top edges outwards and stitch down leaving a short fringe or turn inwards and stitch. Sew the lining to size, leaving the seams outside. Push the lining into the bag. Turn the lining top edge outwards and oversew the bag and lining together. A very thick wool helps to mask the join. Make a broad thick plait long enough to go over the shoulder and down to the bottom corners of the bag (figure 23). Allow at least one-third more length before plaiting. Knot the ends and sew very firmly down sides of bag catching in the lining now and then. Leave a tassel at each corner. Braids woven on Inkle or backstrap looms make a nice finish but the plait is adequate for small bags.

Making cushions and hassocks

Cushion covers should have a lining and a zip fastener, which can all be washed if treated carefully and stretched when damp. A cushion can have a plait round it but is often best left plain. A large tassel on each corner of the cushions, made from the remaining warp ends can be most effective. Upholstered chair seats should be woven from fine tightly spun yarn. If they are to be fixed with nails, machine a strong tape or binding round the edges at the back.

The 50 x 75-cm (20 x 30-in) frame can be used for weaving hassocks for church use in under a week. The usual size, 30 x 22·5 x 7·5 cm (12 x 9 x 3 in) fits well into the frame either horizontally or vertically. The way in which you weave depends on the central de-

sign and also on how good you are at keeping to size. It will be seen that in figure 24 there is less room to spare at the sides. In figure 26 the weaving may get rather tight at the top. Allow at least 2·5 cm (1 in) more overall for take-up in the weaving—more if you are doubtful of keeping the shape true. Use a good linen line for warp spaced according to the thickness of the wool. For A, warp up the full width of the frame; for B about 42·5 cm (17 in) in the middle of the frame.

You will need one or two more cross or shed sticks. It is often a good plan to insert another stick (woven in and out) at the bottom of the frame as it is firmer for beating down. This does, however, lessen the length of warp available for weaving. The second spare stick is needed when the first section of border has been woven (and beaten down). Weave the new stick in and

out of each side, slipping it behind the central woven part. You can then beat the side extensions down to the stick holding it in place.

Choose a small motif for the vertical sides which does not alter too much whether woven sideways or vertically. Weave just the length of the border for 8·75 cm (3½ in), then weave right across the full width. Oversew all edges before cutting off. Turn in and stitch all warp ends and stitch all edges before making up. The bottom of the hassock must be made of very strong cloth or artificial leather. Buy the special firm variety of foam plastic for the stuffing. It can be bought cut to size.

Tapestry is excellent for squab seats for wooden chairs. Turn the sides under to shape, and machine to a strong backing. There is no need to use stuffing. Failed tapestries make ideal mats for dogs or cats.

24 *Horizontal design on frame*

Salish frame

The general principles of the two frames so far mentioned can be applied to a strong wooden bed-frame for weaving rugs. A special room is needed for such a massive piece of equipment. It is possible, however, to build a frame yourself on which anything can be woven up to 150 x 75 cm (5 ft 6 in x 2 ft 6 in) (figure 25). The cost of the timber, bolts and wing nuts is not too great and the measurements need not be exact. However, do not use lighter timber, as strength is essential.

A Salish frame is warped up round a pole tied to the side of the frame to begin with and then pulled across. It can be warped up single-handed in about half an hour. Although a Salish frame is especially useful for tapestry, anything that can be made from 75-cm (30-in) material can be made on it with careful planning (figure 27).

The Salish frame has a tensioner at the top which can be slackened off to allow the work to be pulled round the frame so that it is always at the right height for working. It stands on legs which allow the weaver to sit under it in a comfortable chair. The legs fold flat and the whole thing can fit into an estate car. The dimensions, of course, can be altered to suit the individual.

Before warping up, the tensioner should be above the half-way position. Experience will show, but you need to be able to slack off a lot to pull the work round. Wool will stretch far more than linen warp. The warping pole must be just short enough to pass between the tension bolts. Mark the top of the top beam at 1·25-cm ($\frac{1}{2}$-in) intervals and cut small Vs for the warp to lie in. This helps to keep it spaced. When you have finished weaving, slacken the tension and pull the pole out. The whole thing will drop off.

Making a tabard

When weaving a tabard, it is as well to shorten the warp to avoid wasting yarn. To make a shorter warp, sling a pole below the tension bar.

A tabard can be made in one length with broad bands of white and brown plied warps separated by two thick, almost black warps. The weft of brown grey and white single yarn is woven in diagonal drifts with small random blocks of brilliant colours in Sumak. When finished, the ends are knotted and the garment is washed, stretched and ironed. (The same should be done for cushion covers.)

Cut the material in two, the back about 3·75 cm (1$\frac{1}{2}$ in) longer than the front. When cutting this sort of article always first machine two rows of stitches 1·25 cm ($\frac{1}{2}$ in) apart and cut between them. This prevents fraying.

The neck is cut out in front and the shoulders slightly shaped. Under-arm darts are stitched down. Shoulder seams and the neck edge

25 *Salish frame*

are stitched and pressed open on the right side and covered with a narrow braid sewn down. A plait could be used. Tabards are not seamed at the sides but joined at the waist with braid. The bottom edges can be left as a fringe.

Weaving a rug

A rug woven on this frame can measure 155 x 70 cm (62 x 28 in). A linen warp is used, spaced four to each 2·5 cm (1 in). The weft can be entirely of natural-coloured fleece: black, brown, grey, streaky white and perhaps flecks of sandy-coloured Soay, which is a nice-coloured breed of sheep having very poor wool. Rough-carded kempy wool can be spun into rope thick enough to pass through the spindle eye without being plied. If woven entirely of Kelim weave, like tapestry, the rug will be especially thick and firm. Thick handspun wool is also excellent for pile rugs, woven or stitched.

There is great satisfaction in creating things of beauty from the very beginning and without spending much money on elaborate equipment. Much of the craft-work in this plastic age is rather like making a cake with a packet of cake-mix and an electric mixer. You can eat the cake all right, but it lacks the savour.

26 *Vertical design on frame*

27 *Warping a Salish frame*

tensioner

cross lashing

A triptych of shearing, spinning, dyeing and weaving, designed and woven by K. Smith (overpage)

Books for further reference

On Weaving	Anni Alders	Studio Vista	1966
Techniques of Woven Tapestry	T. Beautlich	Batsford	1967
Techniques of Rug-making	P. Collingwood	Faber	
Techniques of Sprang: plaiting on stretched threads	P. Collingwood	Faber	1974
Spin Your Own Wool and Dye It and Weave It	Molly Duncan	Bell & Hyman	1973
Dyes from Natural Sources	Anne Dyer	Bell & Hyman	1976
Handspinning	Eliza Leadbeater	Studio Vista	1976
Art of Weaving	Else Regensteiner	Studio Vista	1970
Introducing Weaving	P. Shillinglaw	Batsford	1972
The Weaver's Craft	Simpson and Weir	Dryad Press	1969
The Use of Vegetable Dyes	Violetta Thurstan	Dryad Press	1969
Technique of Weaving	J. Tovey	Batsford	1975

That soothing skill of 'fiddling' with twigs...

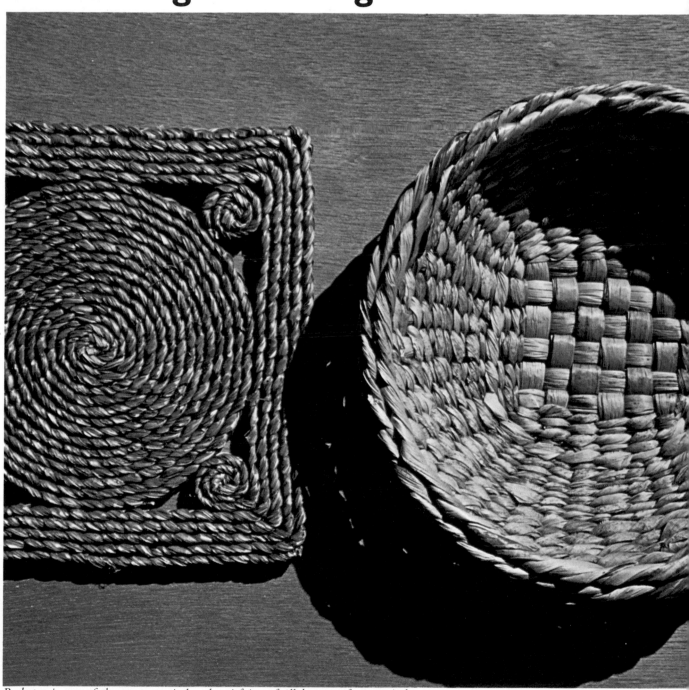

Basketry is one of the most practical and satisfying of all home crafts: practical because its products have a specific everyday use, and satisfying because it means working with natural materials. Ever since discovering that twigs could be worked into useful shapes, man has derived pleasure from basket-making. Here is a basic guide to the craft written by one of its leading present-day practitioners.

The beginnings of basketry

Mankind has always had a tendency to fiddle with bits of grass and twig, sitting in the sun, putting off the next job. It is pleasant to think that basketry may well have evolved from the delight in 'fiddling'. It is certainly one of the very earliest of crafts, pre-dating both weaving and pottery which both developed from it.

Early communities soon began to experiment with materials. The best of these were then developed as man's skill in plant management and harvesting techniques progressed.

Improved strains appeared. Willow was particularly easy to cross-breed and it was no doubt this characteristic which quickly established willow as the main basketry material.

Today willow is available in every colour—black, brown, green, red, yellow, from one-year-old shoots measuring 3 m (10 ft) to dainty garden miniatures.

Willow, nut and rush are now (and probably have been since the Middle Ages) the only 'proper' materials in England. The narrow-leaved willows, called osier, wicker, or withy, are used, while the round-leaved, pithy-centred, sallow or sally willows are ignored.

Wattle means nut; wattle and daub was used in pre-Roman buildings and became the main Saxon building material, used by the rich until Elizabethan times and by poorer country people until this century. It is a mixture of clay or plaster mixed with straw or spear-grass, smoothed on to a nut hurdle.

As trade widened, cane—either the whole creeper (palembang and others) or skinned and machined (centre cane)—from Asia, and willow from France (until the Napoleonic wars put an end to

(Right) Hedger (Far right) Laid hedge (Top) Portable laid hedge.

34

this) were used in basket-making.

English willow beds then came into full production, reaching a peak around 1900 and declining as imports arrived from east Europe and Argentina. During the two world wars, growing was again increased to satisfy war needs, from guardsmen's bearskin frames to parachute hampers. This was especially so in the second world war and because of its war value none was allowed to be used for civilian purposes.

The only professional woman willow basket-maker at that time, Mabel Roffey, experimented with other materials to see if any could be used for basketry, starting with garden shrubs and going on to small woodland trees. She consulted Dr Hutchinson of Kew Gardens, and then set out to teach this new craft of hedgerow basketry to the WI.

Her father had been a woodman and, as a child, she had helped with hurdle-making. This memory may well have been the inspiration for trying out peeled materials other than willow. Today, probably due to the influence of Evelyn Legg in the 1950s, we use hedgerow material, fresh and in its skin for colour.

Rush basketry was revived by Miss Cross of Oxfordshire between the wars, and she wrote the first book on the subject suitable for amateurs, *Rushwork*, which is now unfortunately out of print.

Once you have mastered the basic methods, it is easy to learn more by tracing weaves and borders on existing baskets. This in turn can lead to the study of local and regional shapes, methods and special uses, through local museums. Bas-

(Top) Professional rush-gatherer with scythe and punt

(Far left) Amateurs polling

(Left) Blackthorn and elm hedge which will provide good growth next year

ketry is capable of infinite variations. Once you have mastered the techniques in this book, you will realize how much more there is to discover.

Materials

A word of warning is perhaps necessary at the start. Do not work beyond your strength. If beginners try to handle twigs more than 5 mm ($\frac{1}{5}$ in) thick except as base stakes, (with the exception of garden dogwood which is very pliable) they will end up with a misshapen basket and sore hands.

Bought willow

This is available from some craft shops, or much cheaper in bolts or bundles about 90 cm (36 in) round the base.

Basket willow is usually the Black Maul variety of *Salix triandra* and is usually buff-coloured (skinned after boiling). Brown willow is dried with the skin on, while white willow is peeled but not boiled. They should be stored in a dry placed, preferably standing up.

To prepare, soak in water and then wrap in a damp cloth and polythene sheet to mellow for the following times:
Brown: 1 day soak, 1 day mellow
White: 1 hour soak, 2 hours mellow
Buff: 15-20 minutes soak, 1 hour mellow

Home-gathered hedgerow

Any pliable, un-pithy, one-year-old shoots, free from sideshoots and of good colour. These divide into two types.
Rods Normal, tapering twigs, with a thick butt (bottom) and a thin tip.
Long material Branches that have a constant thickness without much tapering.

Some of the more usual plants to gather are the following.
Garden rods Ornamental willows, dogwood, privet, *Spirea salicifolia*, lilac suckers.
Garden long Weeping willow, broom, jasmine, periwinkle, most hanging creepers.
Native rods Narrow-leaved willows, nut (either shoots on top of hedges, or from the base of woodland plants which are finer and more pliable), elm and lime suckers, dogwood, privet and blackthorn (especially suckers in woods), ash seedlings (handles only), larch.
Native long Bramble, hanging or

(Right) Montbresia leaves and flowers

(Below) Long-leaved sedge

(Above) Weeping willow

(Right) Lilac

(Far right) Hawthorn

ground-growing ivy, clematis, honeysuckle, wild rose, broom.

The best results come from cutting any time between the sap going down in about November (wait for the leaves to fall) until it rises again in about March (watch for the weeping willows to leaf). Cut about 2·5 cm (1 in) from the end of the rod to leave buds for the following year. Sort into thicknesses and types, unless you are cutting for a specific basket, in which case cut about 10 per cent more than you need, to allow for accidents.

Tie into firm bundles and store under a hedge or any shady place out of the wind until ready for use. This may take from three weeks to six months, depending on the weather.

Seering east winds dry it fast, but snow stops all drying. Watch until the string is loose (which indicates how much the twigs have shrunk), the bark dull and wrinkled; the rod must still be pliable, however.

The exceptions to these rules are elm, which can be used in under

six days, and bramble or any peeled material, which can be used at once.

If you want to make the basket and the materials are not quite ready, a few hours indoors will be sufficient. Never keep material indoors unless you are drying it out quickly. Work outdoors if you can. For flower arrangements, containers can be made of fresh material, with its much higher colour. Throw the basket away when it dries and loosens.

De-prickle bramble and rose by pulling through an old jersey. It is usual to peel clematis and honeysuckle to get rid of the bark, which cracks in working. Dip the twigs into boiling water for two seconds (longer and the bark will dye them yellow) and peel towards, not away from, the joint. Other materials can be peeled and stored like willow. Remember, it is easier to peel in March since it is at this time that the sap rises. You can also dry and store rods with the skin on, but the long soaking needed tends to rot the bark.

Annual cutting does not worry

these plants, since they grow new roots with the new top. In many woods the oldest trees are the hazels, which are coppiced every ten years. These can live for up to 400 years. On your own land, cut as and when you like, but do remember the laws of trespass and always ask permission to gather material on someone else's land. Brambles may cover a gap in a hedge and shoots may have been left to grow into trees or to be laid. Always remember that the country is a working area and plants are there because someone has either planted them or spared them, caring that they exist and allowing them to do so for a reason.

Cane

Untie the bundles completely, damp and hang up to dry straight, with their sizes tied to them with dye-fast string. Fine cane can be rolled up into circles, ready for soaking, on labelled loops of string. English sizes (metric in mm under):

0	4	8	12	16	20
1·5	2·25	3	3·75	5	8

40

To prepare:
For metric sizes under 2 mm ($\frac{1}{10}$ in) wrap in damp towel for 15 minutes. Sizes 2-2·5 mm ($\frac{1}{10}-\frac{1}{9}$ in): soak for 2 minutes.
Sizes 2·5-3 mm ($\frac{1}{9}-\frac{1}{8}$ in): soak for 5-10 minutes.
Sizes over 3 mm ($\frac{1}{8}$ in): soak for 10-15 minutes.

Wrap them all in a damp towel for 15 minutes.

If the cane feels dry as you work, wipe with a damp cloth. Use short 1-1·5-m (3-5-ft) lengths to prevent too many whiskers appearing on an overworked cane.

Palembang and other untreated canes need soaking for six hours to three days, depending on ripeness, and should be wrapped in a damp towel and plastic sheet for six hours.

Bought rush
Soft baskets are much easier to make, both in methods and in the behaviour of the materials.

Scirpus lacustris is a giant version of the meadow rush, an unbroken green column with a brown flower tassel on top, not to be confused with sedges (a pampas-grass head and leaves like wheat), or reedmace (which is also called bullrush and has a head like a poker with leaves growing from ground level).

Rushes should feel silky (not crisp like plastic straw which would indicate that they had been cut too late) and be green-gold, without fold-marks on them. Buy both coarse 3-cm (1-in) butt and fine 1-cm ($\frac{1}{2}$-in) butt or below. The length will depend on the water they grew in, not, as in the case of rods, on the butt thickness and will be anything from 1·2-3 m (4-10 ft). Store in a dark, dry place, preferably in a sling of netting.

To prepare, sprinkle liberally with water or soak for one minute. Keep wrapped in a damp cloth and plastic sheet overnight.

Home-gathered material
Rushes grow in many slow, rich streams and lakes; gather when flowering in July. Cut as far below the surface as you can, and keep them straight until they have dried in a dark, airy shed. Turn them frequently. This takes about three weeks. If you are harvesting regularly, only cut an area every other year but do remember to ask permission if it is not your land. Meadow rushes can be treated in the same way and used singly for very small baskets or in handfuls for bigger ones. Gather leaves of reedmace and others from damp places, but not stalks. Gather the leaves of iris, montbresia, red-hot poker and other appropriate plants from the garden.

Leaves can be cut at flowering time for the best colour, or until late winter, when the colour will have changed to brown or cream. The hardening that makes autumn rushes difficult to use does not affect leaves since they crumple. Dry and store them and prepare as rush. Leaves need a minimum of water or they will absorb too much and dry loose.

Before use, wipe each rush leaf to clean it and also to find the weak spots. Stubborn airpockets in rushes can be stabbed with a pin to release any air that has been trapped.

41

Tools and equipment

For all materials

You will require a tape measure and a ruler, a place where you can soak materials, a bath or stream for long willow and big baskets (soapy water does not matter, and hot water halves the soaking time), old cloths, curtains, blankets and a big plastic sheet to wrap things in and scraps of fabric for wiping.

For hard materials

You will also need secateurs, heavy craft knife, a metric knitting needle gauge to check size of rods, a basket-maker's bodkin or well-sharpened 10-cm (4-in) nail, soap to lubricate it, an old tyre-lever wrapped in cloth, or other similar cosh to press rows of weaving down, string and flowerpots or other objects to mould the shapes you require (figure 1).

For cane

In addition, you will need round-nosed pliers for pressing cane so that it will bend easily.

For soft materials

You will also need scissors, moulds to make the basket on, newspaper and adhesive tape for padding the mould, a stone floor, a tile or flat stone about 15-20 cm (6-8 in) across, wrapped in towelling, soft string or strong wool, a threader made from a big sacking needle pushed into a tool handle from a do-it-yourself shop, and a mallet for ironing.

Preparing for action

First of all, take care of your comfort. Choose a chair which will support your back and choose the right height of table so that the arms are not strained. You may like to work on a board placed on a low table, or flat on a high table, or leaning back with the basket in your lap on a plastic apron. In any case, put a sheet on the floor under the chair, because bits tend to scatter (figure 2).

Positioning your hands

The position of every stake must be perfected every time you pass it. There is no way you can force the basket into shape at intervals. So work each weaving stroke in the following manner:

1 Put the left index finger behind the stake about to be woven past, to support it, while the right hand bends the weaver to the back.

2 Move the left thumb forward to hold the next stake back, while the right hand bends the weaver forward against the right thumb held close to the stake.

3 Move the left hand forward, ready for the next stroke, pressing the last weaver down simultaneously.

If any stake is too far forward, push it back and weave tightly in front of it. Do the opposite to a backward-leaning stake. Do not be surprised if your thumbs become flat or a little sore.

In the case of rush, hold the stake up (not to the left) with the left hand while weaving with the right. This prevents it from crumpling down (figure 3).

Aids to shape

Soft baskets are always made on a mould, usually of wood, metal or plastic which can be left in the basket as a lining, or removed. Big butchers' liver tins can be used for waste-paper or small shopping baskets, cooking bowls for shallow dishes, bottles for lampstands (fill with sand and put the wire inside the weaving), bricks or lumps of firewood for plant troughs. If the

1 (Top) Sharpened nail and bodkin (Bottom) Threader for rush work

2 Standard size workboard

3 Correct positions for the hands while weaving

mould is rough or is to be removed, wrap it in several thicknesses of newspaper. When the finished basket is dry, pull the mould out first, then the paper.

Hard baskets are normally worked without a mould, but stakes can be encouraged outwards by putting a flowerpot or similar object inside, or inward by tying them together tightly at the top with a loop of string, or by tying a lampshade ring to several scattered stakes. The secret of good shape is that you should think of each stake as you weave past it.

Planning a basket

1 Find a tin or pot about the size that you want the basket to be, or cut a simple, rough brown paper silhouette, so you can decide the top width, height, angle of sides and whether they are to be curved or straight. Stare at it until you are satisfied and then keep it in mind all the time you are making the basket.

2 Calculate the number of side stakes from the top spacing as it is most important to have the stakes the right distance apart when working the border.

Hard baskets Measure five or six stakes at border thickness to give the spacing. Divide this into the distance round the top (counting three times the top width of the silhouette as the distance round). Adjust to the nearest number divisible by four. If bystaking, lay seven stakes together.

Example: Size 8 cane, 3 mm ($\frac{1}{8}$ in), for a 20-cm (8-in) diameter basket. The distance apart is 6 x 3 mm (6 x $\frac{1}{8}$ in) which is 1·8 cm ($\frac{3}{4}$ in). Divide this into 3 x 20 cm (8 in) for the top circumference: 3 x 20 ÷ 1·8 or 3 x 20 x 10 ÷ 18 = 33$\frac{1}{3}$ (or 3 x 8 ÷ $\frac{3}{4}$ = 32 as the conversion is only a rough guide). In either case 32 is the nearest number divisible by 4, so you need 32 stakes.

Cut the right number of side stakes, the slant height of the basket plus one-third base diameter plus amount for chosen border, making

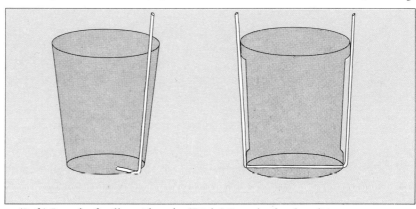

4 (Left) Length of willow side stake (Right) Length of rush stake

Table I

Hedgerow comments		small mm (in)	medium baskets mm (in)	large mm (in)
Side stakes and bystakes	Strong, good tempered rods. Choose first	2·5 ($\frac{1}{10}$)	3 ($\frac{1}{8}$)	4·5 ($\frac{1}{5}$)
Base stakes	Thickest, strongest do not bend much	3·5 ($\frac{1}{7}$)	4 ($\frac{1}{6}$)	6 ($\frac{1}{4}$)
Base weavers	Start with long material; not as strong as stakes	2 ($\frac{1}{12}$)	2·5 ($\frac{1}{10}$)	3 ($\frac{1}{8}$)
Walers	Long rods or long material; weaker than stakes	2 ($\frac{1}{12}$)	2·5 ($\frac{1}{10}$)	3 ($\frac{1}{8}$)
Side weavers	Thinner than walers; no need to bend much	1$\frac{3}{4}$ ($\frac{1}{14}$)	2 ($\frac{1}{12}$)	2·5 ($\frac{1}{10}$)
Handle	Strong, thick, even width, can be two years old; usually nut, ash or willow	3 ($\frac{1}{8}$)	5 ($\frac{1}{5}$)	8 ($\frac{1}{3}$)
Handle winders	Finest, longest, smooth surface, can be long material	1·5 ($\frac{1}{16}$)	2 ($\frac{1}{10}$)	3 ($\frac{1}{8}$)

Table 2   Lengths of materials required

	For shopping basket	**For posy basket**
Base stakes	8, 5 mm ($\frac{1}{5}$ in) thick, 22·5 cm (9 in) long	6, 3 mm ($\frac{1}{8}$ in) thick, 10 cm (4 in) long
Side stakes	32, 4 mm ($\frac{1}{8}$ in) thick 25 cm (10 in) from butt, at least 45 cm (18 in) long	24, 2 mm ($\frac{1}{10}$ in) thick 15 cm (6 in) from butt, at least 30 cm (12 in) long
Bystakes	32, same size, can be a bit shorter	24, same size, can be a bit shorter, or 15 cm (6 in) if not in border
Base weavers	a good handful, 3 mm ($\frac{1}{4}$ in) thick at butt of rods (or thinner if long material)	a small handful, 2 mm ($\frac{1}{10}$ in) thick or less
Walers	About 25 m (78 ft), 3 mm ($\frac{1}{10}$ in) thick, long material	About 11 m (36 ft), 2 mm ($\frac{1}{10}$ in) thick, long material
Side weavers	Roughly 50 x diameter of circle to be waled is safe for three rows of waling. 36 x diameter can be managed.	
	up to 3 mm ($\frac{1}{10}$ in thick)	2 mm ($\frac{1}{17}$ in) thick

If the rods are long enough to go all round the basket, estimate the amount by laying the rods closely together until they roughly measure the height of the basket. (Unfaded hedgerow will need to be twice the basket height to allow for shrinkage.)

In the case of shorter rods, allow proportionately more. Then add some for luck.

	For shopping basket	**For posy basket**
Handle	8 mm ($\frac{1}{3}$ in) thick, 1 m (3 ft) long plus two liners, 25 cm (9 in) long.	4 mm ($\frac{1}{6}$ in), 45 cm (18 in) long plus two liners 12·5 cm (5 in) long
Handle winders	about 12, as thin as possible 75 cm (30 in) long.	about 10, as thin as possible, 40 cm (15 in) long

Suggested colour schemes for hedgerow baskets

Shopping basket

Stakes	peeled nut or willow	garden dogwood	green or brown willow
Wale	ivy	red bramble or peeled willow	bramble or rose
Weave	weeping willow	garden dogwood	elm or larch

Posy basket

Stakes	blackthorn suckers	red willow	elm
Wale	peeled honeysuckle	red bramble	privet
Weave	broom (green and white)	black sally (red or rusty)	*Spirea salicifolia* (brown and gold)

5 Handle tied up for drying

6 Second stage of making base

7 Base cross fiinished

8 Ready to start weaving base
First stroke of pairing weave

First rows of base weaving

sure, with anything but cane, that the thickness where the border turns down is manageable. If not, cut off the butt. It is usual not to trim the unwanted length off the top of rods until the border is reached, to make the mending of broken stakes easier (figure 4).

Cut a quarter as many base stakes, as long as the base diameter plus 2.5 mm (1 in) and about one and a half times as fat as the side stakes. For instance, 3-mm ($\frac{1}{8}$-in) side stakes need 4·5-mm ($\frac{1}{6}$-in) base stakes.

Soft baskets The stakes are much closer, with at most a quarter of the flattened stake width between them. So you must determine the top circumference (three times the top diameter), halve it (because stakes go right round the basket) and spread out enough rushes to measure nearly that distance. The rushes should be cut long enough to go down one side, across the bottom, and up the other side, plus two border amounts. They should also be flattened.

3 Plan the bands of weaving on the sides by laying strips of newspaper on the design, remembering how high the border will be, and allowing for the usual three rows of waling top and bottom.

4 Mix the colours of hedgerow materials, or willow with cane or hedgerow. When you can, mix thicknesses: this can be done with soft materials or with hedgerow, where strength does not always match thickness. (A wild dogwood stake is stronger than a garden dogwood weaver twice as thick.

Order of working hard materials

Gather or buy and sort your materials with the following thicknesses in mind. Remember home-gathered materials will shrink, so cut a bit thicker than you want.

Always prepare more than is needed, to avoid holdups while

45

another piece is soaking. Hedgerow baskets can be helped out, if all else fails, by the use-at-once materials such as bramble and peeled rods. Check each rod before you use it for breaks or snags. If at any stage you are struggling to control it, either the material is too heavy for you, or has not been soaked enough. Never keep materials damp between working sessions, in case mildew develops, but wipe or wrap them in a damp cloth if they get too dry while working.

To help you make the 28-cm (11-in) diameter willow or hedgerow shopping basket, or the 12·5-cm (5-in) cane or hedgerow posy basket, see requirements in Table 2.

Making a basket

1 Slype (carve off to a long tapering point) both ends of the handle and one end of each liner. Bend the handle (soaked unless hedgerow) round a tin or pot the size of the basket top, and tie with the legs at the angle to which the basket will be woven. Dry. It is a good idea to have a supply of dry handles, cut about three and a half times the diameter of the mould, of various useful sizes (figure 5).

2 Prepare (soak or fade) the base stakes and base weavers.

3 Pierce half the stakes in the middle with the bodkin, pushing them to the top of the spike to make a split. Push the bodkin sideways in the split to widen it. Sharpen one end of the others and push the first one in where the bodkin was and move it to the other end of the slit. Put in the second one, remove the bodkin and replace it with this stake. Add the rest between these two. Bend all into a slight saucer shape (figures 6, 7).

4 If weaving with rods, push the sharpened butts of two long thin ones into the split and bring one of them forward into the next gap. If using long material, bend carefully into an uneven hairpin (to stagger the joins) and slip round one bundle of stakes (figure 8).

5 Starting with weavers coming out to left and right of the upward pointing bundle of stakes, begin to weave. Take the left weaver across front of upward bundle, over other weaver, behind right-hand bundle and back to the side of the base facing you. Then turn the base so that what was the right-hand bundle becomes the upward one. Repeat until you estimate there is space to open up the stakes (three or four rows) (figure 9).

6 Continue pairing but now go between each stake (or, in the case of four stakes in a bundle, you can split them into pairs for a few rounds and then single them). Use

(Right) The completed base

(Below) The pairing principle

9 Pairing weave started

10 Stakes opened up evenly

11 Base stakes cut off, side stakes inserted, one pricked for turning up

the bodkin and your hands to make the stakes bend apart and to push the weavers down. Weave in two movements (to the back, to the front) for a few rows to get into the spaces. Aim at having the stakes evenly spaced by row ten, then concentrate on the saucer shape by bending each stake down a bit as you weave it. Some people weave over their knee, others clasp the work to their chest to achieve this shape. An average 20-cm (8-in) base should be 1 cm ($\frac{1}{2}$ in) high in the middle; more for hedgerow. This saucering makes the basket stand well and prevents the bottom from falling out (figure 10).

7 When you are 1 cm ($\frac{1}{2}$ in) from the end of the stakes, fasten off by slipping the last weaver into the previous row. Dry completely, including hedgerow.

Weaving a practice frame

Glue a piece of corrugated paper 3 x 20-25 cm (1 x 8-10 in) between two pieces of stiff cardboard.

Put glue on the ends of matches and push them about 1-1·5 cm ($\frac{3}{8}-\frac{5}{8}$ in) into the corrugations about 1·5-2 cm ($\frac{5}{8}-\frac{3}{4}$ in) apart.

Practise weaves on this with as many different-coloured wools as there are in the stroke, following the directions in the text, until you can do them without thinking. You will then be able to concentrate on the control of the materials and the shape of the basket when you start on the real thing.

8 Upset the basket. Make a 2·5-cm (1-in) slype on the butt end of all the side stakes. Soak the bottom quarter (not hedgerow). Prepare enough material for three rows of waling (40-50 x diameter).

9 Cut off the ends of the base stakes, one at a time (preferably in a haphazard order, otherwise the weaving could twist into an oval) right against or even inside the weaving. Push a side stake in each side, cut surface against the base stakes, until they nearly reach the middle. If difficult, push a hole with the soaped bodkin (figure 11).

10 When all are in, trim the ends of weaving, except the last one, so that they lie neatly on a stake. Use secateurs held flat against the base. Trimming with a knife is for experts.

11 Lay the base, dome up, on a board, and prick right through each stake with the bodkin where

Pricking through stakes before upsetting the basket

it emerges from the weaving. Cane is usually nipped with pliers, but do remember that it is also too easy to nip them right through. Fold each stake upwards, supporting base with other hand. Ensure bend is sharp to avoid rounded base edge. Release (figure 12).

12 Pick up all the stakes, opposites first, and hold them near the top, over the exact centre of the base. Tie tightly. Turn over and check that the stakes have bent close to the weaving, and add more pairing if necessary (figure 12).

13 Trim the thin tips off the first three walers and slip into the base to the left of three sidestakes. Do three rows of waling with the first row over the edge of the basket. Step-up or not, according to choice. If you are not doing a step-up, end

12 *Stakes upset ready for waling*

13 *Handle liner in place*

48

when you reach the first tips after the three rows, to get a gentle petering out, or use the same rods to start the side weaving if suitable. To upset a bowl-shape, just turn over and weave after stage 10, bending the stakes up to resemble the curve of a very steep saucer until the angle of the sides is right. Tie up if you wish to do so.

14 Untie the stakes and you will find that the shape should hold.

15 Bystake, if wanted, push the butts into the weave to the right of

each stake. Then treat the two stakes as one. Professionals put to the left if the bystakes are being woven into the border to protect the stake, but to the right if they are being cut off before the border.

16 Except for hedgerow, in which any tightening of the finished basket is welcome, set the handle liners to the left of two opposite stakes and, again, treat the liner and stake as one when weaving (figure 13).

17 Work the sides. Rand, slew or pair for cane or long material. However, these weaves become very uneven with rods, which are

usually worked in French, mock French or English rand or slew. Aim at opening up to the planned top width of the basket by the time you are half way up the sides and then go straight since this is currently considered to make a better shape. Perfect the angle and spacing of each stake as you pass it.

Different weaves

Baskets often have a decorative band just below the top waling, slewing above randing, chain pair, or a change of hedgerow colour. A narrow band of French randing

Up-setting

with alternate coloured rods gives you a pattern of upward stripes.

Rand One weaver at a time; but since there is usually an even number of stakes, you must start a second weaver at the opposite side of the basket going in front of the stakes, that the first weaver will go behind. Then let them chase each other round the basket. Weave behind and in front of each stake in turn, making sure the weaver does all the bending and that it is not pushing the stakes out of place. Randing (or pairing in soft materials) can be done in jumping ones and twos (figure 14).

Slew Randing with two or more weavers as one ribbon.

Mock French rand Find two fewer weavers than stakes, put tips together and cut off at butt end to length of the shortest. This should make them about the same thickness. Put the first butt in behind a stake, and weave one rand-stroke (in front of second stake, behind third stake and out to the right side). Put the second weaver in, starting one stake to the left of the previous start, and work one rand-stroke; add all the rest, each one to the left of the last. This will leave a gap in the ring of weavers. Do one rand-stroke with the weaver to the

left of the space. Repeat until the tips are reached. If the basket is not high enough, add a row of waling if you like, and another band of mock French. Two bands, one starting with the tips (a tricky operation) and the other, with the butts, look attractive (figure 15).

French rand Start as for mock French, but have as many weavers as there are stakes. The first weavers have to be lifted up to enable the last two to be set in. Start a row of weaving anywhere, and work as before. You will see that the first

two strokes produce two weavers in each of two gaps; the row is finished when the bottom pairs have been woven on, leaving a weaver in each space again. Work as many rows as the rod length allows. Start a new band as before, or with mock-wale, where each stake is set in in front of two stakes and behind one.

French and mock French rand Both can be worked with two or more rods at a time, as for slewing.

English rand Find as many weavers as stakes, and make sure they are at

Posy basket 15·25 cm (6 in) long, blackthorn stakes, wild broom randing, peeled honeysuckle wale, three-rod border

14 *Two rand weavers started*

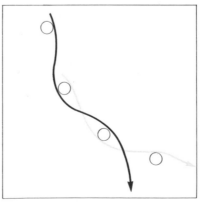

15 *Mock French rand; first two weavers in position*

16 *English rand, first weavers in position*

least one and a quarter times the circumference of the basket, and with a
butt much thinner than the stakes.
Take the shortest (the basket gets
bigger as it rises), rand it in, starting
with the butt and stopping when
the tip reaches the butt again. Start
the second weaver one stake to the
right and repeat. Continue until
all weavers are used and there is a
butt behind every stake. If the basket
is too high to allow another complete set, work with one-third the

English rand

17 *How to pair*

18 *How to wale*

number, starting behind every third stake, or change weave (figure 16).

Pair Two weavers. An easy weave for adjusting untidy stakes, which is why it is used on bases. Start by putting the rods behind, or into the weaving beside two neighbouring stakes. Take the left one and do a rand-stroke. Repeat with the other, which has now become the left one (figure 17).

Chain pair A decorative variation mostly used for cane or soft baskets. Do a row of normal pair, then a row of pairing where each weaver goes under, not over, the other worker.

Wale Three weavers. A strong weave, which holds the top and bottom of a basket together, and protects the stakes from knocks. Set the ends into the weaving beside three neighbouring stakes, or behind them. Take the left weaver in front of two stakes, behind one and out on the right side, crossing over the other weavers as you go. Repeat with what has now become the left-hand weaver. Waling can be done with four or more, for thick lines, forward to the next empty space (figure 18).

French wale For the first row after upsetting set in four (or six) weavers, weave as normal. Each weaver, as it moves, goes under two and over one (or under three, over two) of the other weavers instead of over them all.

Chain wale Alternate rows of normal wale and wale taking each weaver under the others, instead of over.

Step-up In cane and sometimes with long material, it is neater to complete each row of wale rather than to spiral up regardless. Work normally until the right-hand weaver is in the gap to the left of the beginning of the row; then work a normal wale-stroke with the right, middle and left weaver, in that order. Start the next row normally. To finish: at the same stage, work as before, but bring the ends out under the start of the row, instead of on top. To step up chain-wale,

use the same idea but go in under the start of the row and come out above (figure 19).

Fitch This leaves the stakes uncovered. It is quick to do but is not hard-wearing. The stakes can be left straight, perhaps thickened by pushing extra ones into the spaces in the waling above and below. Or the proper stakes or the bystakes (often added on each side) can be

crossed. Long fitch often has rows of pairing at intervals to secure it, and it is perhaps best, especially with rush, to put an extra twist between each stake. A folded newspaper strip woven in is useful for keeping such rows equally spaced. This can easily be removed while still wet, when the basket is finished. Extra bystakes added for fitch can be cut off before the border, woven

19 *Stepping up in middle and at end of a band of waling*

20 *Variations of trac border*

21 *How to work a three-rod border*

52

into the border or used for an extra border on the outside or inside to make a ridge for a lid or easy lifting of waste-paper baskets.

Making a basket (continued)

18 When the sides are woven, dry the basket off and push the weaving well down. This cannot be done with hedgerow unless the stakes are peeled and will soak successfully.

19 Cut bystakes off, if not wanted in the border. They are the right-hand one of each pair. Trim the stakes to the required length for the border if you cannot soak the whole length.

20 Soak the stakes down to the second row of waling, upside down in a bucket with a stone on its bottom to keep it down.

21 Border. Start with the stake one or two to the left of the handle liner, or with a stake which has three or four really pliable, good-tempered stakes to its left. If hard to work, soak longer.

Choose type of border wanted.

Slewing

Different borders

Trac The length of stake needed depends on the type of trac worked. Decide on a pattern, see how many stakes it passes, measure the distance and add a bit for luck. If your stakes are not long enough, pick another pattern. How far above the waling the stake will need pricking or nipping to bend down also depends on the pattern: count the moves ('in front of one' or 'in front of three' are both one move) and bend that number of stake-thicknesses up from the weaving. Bend over the first stake and weave the pattern to the right, being careful that it bends and does not push the other stakes out of position. End on either the inside or outside, as you like. Weave the next stake to the right in the same pattern, and continue until you are bending the stake on which the first one ends. If you have judged the height right, this should fold over a tight-packed border below it. If it does not, undo it and adjust the height. Continue until the last few are threaded in under the first one, to keep the pattern. Be careful not to crack the stakes; try to keep them bent in a curve and weave back and forward in two moves. Use the bodkin and soap to make spaces to weave through (figure 20).

Three-rod This is one of a group with many versions, depending on how many stakes are taken down before the first down-stake is brought forward, whether the stakes are taken behind one or two, and how long the follow-on is. The normal version uses the distance between seven stakes (ten for the border with follow-on). Squeeze or prick one stake thickness above the wale. To make the join easy, find three 20-cm (8-in) pieces of the same thickness as the stakes. Put the first waste piece behind stake B, with both its ends on the right side. Bring stake A down to the right of it, between stakes B and C. Lay the second waste piece behind C, and bring B down beside

54

Parts of a basket

handle stake

handle winder

top wale

peg

side stake

bottom wale

22 Handle, pegged and being wrapped

23 Two joins in pairing

it. The third waste piece goes behind D, and C comes down to join it. The rest of the way round, take the right-hand stake from the most left-hand pair (A) into the next space (between E and F) and bring the left standing stake (D) down beside it. Keep these two stakes flat, not piled up. When you reach the join, thread W and Z under A, through where the first waste piece is, removing it as you go. Y replaces the second waste piece and Z the third waste piece (figure 21).

If there is a gap between the border and the wale, work a follow-on. This means pushing each end through to the wrong side, one, two or three stakes ahead of where it is now, always going over (or under) the other stake-ends on the way.

22 Dry the basket completely.

23 If you have produced a wobbly, rounded bottom (which beginners often do) add a false bottom. Slype and soak as many short stakes (ten in 25 cm/10 in for a big basket) as there are side stakes, but a bit finer. Turn the basket upside down and set the stakes in wherever seems best in the waling in order for them to be reasonably evenly spaced.

Fine cane bowls

Do a few rows of weaving if necessary and turn down a border.

24 Soak the handle winders. Find a dry handle-bow of the right size and put it round the basket to see how high you want it. The lower it is, the stronger, and it is rare now to see a handle much more than three-quarters of the top diameter above the basket. Cut off the ends to reach almost to the bottom of the basket and slype very well, so that the point is sharp and the sides smooth. Remove the liners and put

55

(Above) Finishing border on
cardinalis willow basket

the handle in, pushing a little on each side in turn. Secure by pushing the bodkin through the handle at an angle, somewhere in the wale, remove and slip in a peg (a burnt match or a trimmed butt). Cut this off flush with the weaving. The handle can be left like this or it can have a wrapped end, or be wrapped all over (figure 22).

For willow or hedgerow, find ten or a dozen very fine rods at least one and a half times the handle bow, slype their ends and soak (not hedgerow). Push three or four in beside the handle in a flat group,

(Left) A sampler basket lid showing a variety of weaves. How many can you identify?

usually on the left. Keeping them in a smooth ribbon, wrap them across the front of the handle to the right, round the back to the left and round again until they reach the top. Repeat on the other side. Let the bundles pass each other and wind down the other side to the border. If there are gaps, add more, equally on both sides, and wind in so the handle is completely covered with no crossed rods. If the tips are long enough, take them through the border and over in a single or double cross before weaving them away into the wale, or wherever you can. If they are too

short, leave them down beside the handle or weave them away. Bind them into place with a new thin rod, set in with the others, taken a little way up the handle, turned sideways and wrapped down. Weave the tip away to fasten it off.

Cane handles can be covered in the same way, using one long piece and chasing back and forth until it is used up. Then tuck the end into the border and add a new one.
25 Trim all ends inside and outside the basket. Dry off completely.
26 Cane baskets should be soaked and then have their whiskers singed off over burning methylated spirits in a tin lid. Candles can stain the cane, and so do not use. Brush the ash off with a clothes-brush.

Wooden bases

Bought bases are usually for 2·5-mm ($\frac{1}{10}$-in) cane, much too fine for proper baskets and too close to bystake. For hedgerow and willow, it is better to make your own. Use wood or plywood, thick enough to take the wear that will be imposed on it. Draw a line 1 cm ($\frac{3}{8}$ in) from the edge all round, and mark the spacing of the holes, bearing in mind the border widths. Make two holes near the corner, rather than one corner hole, as they weave better. Drill big enough holes through the base and into a piece of scrap wood underneath to avoid splits. The wood can be stained with floorstain or vegetable dye (purple fruit juice gives a good purple-grey).

Always use peeled stakes, as inserting tears the bark. Soak normally and then wipe off loose water which can stain the wood. Push the tip through from below and pull up until it wedges. (Cane is pushed through from the top.) Turn the base over and work a border, pushing stakes up for easy finishing off. Trim.

Turn the base over and work the sides, getting the stakes upright as quickly as possible by firm handling, as the border underneath will probably leave them leaning badly.

Joins in hard materials

In pair and wale, leave the run-out end on the right side and continue working normally until you need it. Then slip the new weaver in beside the old one and continue. It is easier to slip it in to the right of the old one, but for a better finish it goes to the left, under the old one and crosses over its end on its first stroke.

For rand and slew, leave the end on the inside and lay the new one in where it would have come forward.

Joins in hard and soft materials

Stagger joins whenever you can, even if it means some waste. Always join butt to butt and tip to tip. Leave all ends about 2 cm (1 in) long until you are ready to trim them properly.

Joins in soft materials

Nearly always, the join is inside leaving a reasonably long end which can be pushed down between the weaving and the mould. The tips can be overlapped and worked together for a few strokes (figure 23).

Broken stakes in soft material

Soak a new piece and tie a knot in its end. Push the threader a reasonable way down the weaving over where the broken stake is, and pull the new piece up to take its place, with the knot against the weave.

(Above) Wooden base basket, peeled willow stakes, black willow bystakes, wild rose wale

(Top right) Garden dogwood fruit plate, pair, wale, three-rod border

(Bottom right) Basket made on stakes stuck in the ground to keep hay from being trampled into the mud by cattle

Cut off the knot in the final trim.

Broken stakes in hard material

If the break is near the top of the weaving, slype the broken-off piece and push in a short way, to the left. If this will make the stake too short for the border, add a new piece.

Methods for making soft baskets

The exact thickness of materials is less important in making soft baskets because there is not an equivalent difference in strength between thick and thin. Aim at thick stakes, fine walers and finer side weavers, unless doing check weave.

1 Find a mould. If it is to be ultimately removed, wrap it in four layers of newspaper; if not, neaten rough edges of tins with pliers or file, and paint with enamel to prevent rusting.

2 Dampen and mellow enough material for the time available.

3 Work on a damp towel over a plastic bag or apron on the table while making the base, and later on your lap. Keep a wet rag for wiping the material before you start and whenever it feels dry.

4 Measure the width of the base, then subtract 2·5 cm (1 in) for straight-sided moulds. Cut the stakes twice the height plus the base width plus twice the border allowance—10 cm (4 in) for a simple trac to 20 cm (8 in) for three-rod and lay them under the brick until they measure the right amount in the middle. If the rush stakes are long, lay them alternately top and tail to even out the border. Use leaves about four times as thick as the weavers will be, by working with several together, preferably laid with their stalk-ends well overlapping. Cut the same measurement (not the same number of stakes unless they are all of the same thickness) to go the other way.

5 Find the centre of the stakes by folding, and put the brick to one side of it. Pick up every other stake and lay one of the other set across those still on the table. Put down the raised stakes and pick up the others right against the cross stake. Lay the next one in (top to tail, if long). Continue, making sure that the weaving is tight and square by pulling each stake as you lay it down and tucking the laid-in stake

60

firmly under it. When half is woven, move the brick on to this and then weave the other half out from the centre (figure 24).

6 Remove the brick and lay the mould on. Unweave the corners, turning these stakes diagonally out, until the woven area is 1 cm (½ in) smaller than the mould all the way round (figure 25).

7 Put the stone back on. Fold a fine weaver into a hairpin with well-staggered ends and slip the loop over the left-hand stake pointing away from you. Pair along the side, turn the base and continue for two rows, keeping the shape round and the weave tight by pulling each stake gently outward and each weaver inwards.

8 Put the mould upside down and lift the base on to it without turning it over. Tie it on with a cross of wool right round the mould. Work

another row or two and tie on again. Work until just over the edge of the mould.

9 Upset by folding the stakes up the side of the mould, and weave three rows of wale with the basket in your lap on a plastic apron and wet towel, its base towards you. It is usual to add a third weaver to the present two and, if working with leaves, thicken each bundle a little.

10 Pair, chain pair, wale, chain wale or fitch are good weaves for the sides, or rush check weave,

24 Second stake inserted in rush base

25 Rush base corners uncrossed and start of pairing weave

26 Start and finish of a rush handle

27 Opening up bowl doubled stakes

which is quick but not hard-wearing. Weave as for rand but choose a rush nearly as thick as the stakes and keep it flat. Start and finish by cutting a long taper to avoid a sudden hump. If you have an even number of stakes (and, barring accidents, you should have) start another on the opposite side (see rand). Join by overlapping two ends for two or three stokes. This weave can also be done with leaves.

Stop weaving the sides when you reach a point when what remains to be woven is equivalent to the depth of the bottom waling if the mould is to stay in, earlier if not.

11 Three rows of waling, stepping up if required.

12 Soak the stakes if they need it (and they should) and work a simple trac or three-rod border. A trac of 'in front, behind, in front', well pulled down, looks like a plait. The first turns can be loose, for easier completion, and pulled tight afterwards. Trim, leaving at least 1·5 cm ($\frac{1}{2}$ in) sticking out or it may become loose.

13 Remove the wool. Trim outside. Roll on the table or tap gently with a mallet to smooth the surface.

14 Add a handle if required, before or after removing the mould. Thread three long rushes through the border, bring them together and plait. Fasten off by threading half the ends each way through the border on the opposite side and weave the ends away (figure 26).

15 Dry it completely. Remove the mould if desired, trim inside.

Other shapes of soft baskets

Bowls It is easier to start with enough stakes to do the border at the right spacing, rather than add them, but you will not want as many in the base weave. So cut enough stakes to flatten to a size, one and a quarter times the top diameter. Divide into two equally wide bundles and decide by how much you want to narrow it. This

is done by weaving two stakes as if they were one as often as required. As the bowl progresses and gaps appear between stakes, separate the stakes, four equally spaced pairs each time, until they are all single, well before the border. As the inside of a bowl is visible, consider a pattern in the centre, woven with the stakes (figure 27).

Square and oblong baskets Weave the base as before but almost the size of the mould and do not undo the corners. Tie on at once. Remember the stakes will be two different lengths.

Big baskets If the long stakes are too thin by the border, make all stakes double, laid butt to tip, and work as one throughout.

Mending

Avoid central heating. Rush loves damp floors. Throw all your baskets out in the rain or into the bath every three months to prolong life.

Most mending is done by removing the damaged piece and replacing it by normal methods. This group includes stakes broken in the border, broken handles and soft basket stakes broken in the side or base (figure 28).

If, in a hand basket, a lot of border stakes are broken, at least some of the stakes will have to be replaced right down to the middle of the base or the basket will not stand hard use. This is most easily done by removing the old stakes one at a time, pushing a new one up the space, with its butt already bent, ready to slip into the base as the stake finishes its journey. Or glue a new one to the old stake, cut off half way up the basket.

A side stake broken in the weaving can have another slipped in to its left all the way down the basket. Broken weaving needs unravelling until the trimmed-off ends are well staggered, and new pieces woven in.

Exhibition tips

Rush Store materials and baskets in the dark to keep their colour.

(Above) Palembang cane basket base; note mark at centre where bodkin held it to workboard
Pair, rand, wale with five and three weavers

(Right) Clothes basket of coarse cane, plain and pattern rand, chain pair and wale

Exhibit in their first year only. Never use a twice-soaked rush as it will have lost colour.

Willow Soak the day before the exhibition to tighten up the weave.

Hedgerow is for fun. Never exhibit it, or, if you do, make it within a week of the exhibition and keep it outdoors. Last year's hedgerow baskets will dry loose. Push the weaving down and weave in a few extra rows.

Utter failures Use in the garden, turned upside down over alpines as frost protection.

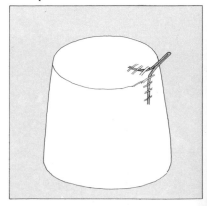

28 Mending a broken side stake

Books for further reference

Rush and Leafcraft	Germaine Brotherton	Batsford	1977
Canework	C. Crampton	Dryad Press	1961
Willow Basket Work	A. J. Knock	Dryad Press	1958
Baskets and Basketry	Dorothy Wright	David & Charles	1972

Suppliers

Basketmakers' Association
Barbara Maynard (Chairman)
Saxon House   Icketon   Saffron Walden   Essex

Rushes
Metcalfe-Arnold   Wildcroft   Holywell   St Ives   Hunts.

Willow
Jacob, Young & Westbury   Bridge Road   Haywards Heath   Sussex.

The myth that made an ancient craft

Ever since man began to till the soil, corn dollies have been part of harvest mythology. The skill was handed down from father to son and for many centuries was a vital part of rural lore in all lands where corn was grown, the making of the 'dolly' ensuring that the following year's harvest would be bountiful. Corn marquetry—the inlaying of pieces of corn for decorative effect—is a closely related activity which is equally absorbing and also practised worldwide. Here these traditional skills are explained in words and pictures by an expert in the craft.

The origin of corn dollies

Ceremonies connected with the harvest of crops have been practised for centuries all over the world. Most have been associated with fertility rites and the worship and placation of the goddess of the corn. It is known that wheat and barley were growing wild in the Near and Middle East around 8000 BC. The earliest farmers discovered that these grasses yielded dry fodder for animals and when bruised and sodden, food also for man.

The women in these small early farming communities used a primitive method of agriculture. They would roughly prepare the ground with a notched stick as their only implement. When the earth's goodness at one place has been exhausted, these early farmers would move on to the next site. Some followed a migrational urge to the west, but others settled in the fertile valley of the Nile, where Emmer wheat seeds have recently been found preserved in grain pits. In colder climates, oat seeds from Persia and rye from the highest slopes of the Hindu Kush were successfully sown and harvested.

Nothing was known of seed germination and so it was thought that a goddess had control of the fertility of the field and of the well-being of the crops. It was believed that it was within the goddess's power to give a good or a bad harvest. Sacrifices were made to her and also to images made in the primitive conceptualized likeness of the goddess. These images were usually made of straw, often taken from the last sheaf. The design over many years became by tradition a symbol of the goddess in the corn.

It is this idol or image of the goddess that is the origin of the corn dolly that survives today. The goddess had a variety of names—Isis in Egypt, Demeter in Greece, Ceres in Italy; local names included Harvest Bride, Harvest Queyn, Bride of the Corn and many others.

Over the centuries these early nomadic farmers migrated to southern England and Scandinavia in about 4000 BC, taking with them their superstitions and their beliefs in their gods and goddesses.

It was the memory of this ancient pagan worship and of the placation of the goddess that inspired the ceremonies connected with the harvest in remote areas of England, Scotland and Ireland as late as the early nineteenth century. The corn dolly was considered to be the resting place of the goddess or spirit of the corn after the crop was cut. It was preserved and held in reverence until the following year, when a new one was made, so ensuring the fertility and continuity of harvest.

The art of corn dolly-making was handed down from father to son, occasionally from mother to daughter, and there are accounts of small farming communities taking part in time-honoured customs of which the original meaning had long been forgotten.

One of these ceremonies is recorded in William Hone's *Everyday Book* published in 1827. It was called 'Crying the neck' and came from Devon. The 'neck' was the name given to the corn doll in that county:

'At the end of harvest, the men and women stand round an old man who has plaited the "neck" or sheaf from the best ears of corn. They all chant "Wee-en, way-en" mournfully as he first touches the ground with the neck, then raises it on high while all shout for joy.'

This curious chant could be interpreted as 'We're in' or 'The harvest is in'.

Sometimes a young girl would take the principal part in the ceremony and, sitting high on the last wagon, would carry the corn baby.

In other accounts a magnificent Harvest Queen was carried on to the field with a sickle under her arm and with 'music and much clamour' was taken home at night.

Mrs Leather's *Folk Lore* has a record of 'Crying the mare' in Herefordshire. A small patch of corn was left standing in the field to represent the mare. Legs were indicated by tying this into four bunches. Sickles, held by their points, were thrown to cut the legs of the mare. This was made even more difficult for the thrower, as he had to have his back to the mare and had to throw from between his legs. The man who succeeded was the guest of honour at the harvest supper. The final stage was the weaving of the straw of the mare into some form of straw trophy.

Straw figures from the northern counties were sometimes dressed in a child's frock and bonnet, and some people think the name corn dolly could have originated from this custom.

That there were two ways of considering the corn spirit is clear from these accounts. In some parts of Wales the corn dolly was called a 'hag'. She would be taken by a fast runner to any neighbouring farmer who had not finished his harvest. The runner would try to arrive unobserved and throw the straw hag under the headman's

sickle from behind the hedge. This involved a certain amount of risk, since if he was caught, he could be bound hand and foot, and left in the field, or thrown in the river.

There was obviously a fear of being the last farmer to possess the corn hag as she was considered to be unlucky.

'Y Gaseg Fedi', the Harvest Mare was also recorded in Wales. This was basically like the Herefordshire ceremony, with the exception that after the legs of the mare had been cut, there was a free fight for possession. The successful reaper was the one who ran first to the farmhouse, having dodged the girls lying in wait to pour water on him, and he became the hero of the evening. (The water was originally considered a charm for good rainfall the following year.) But, successful or not, the reaper demanded kisses all round and in every case the mare was hung up for all to see.

The 'maighdean bhuana' or corn maiden and the 'cailleagh' or corn

mother are names given to the two corn dollies, symbolizing the new and the old corn in Argyll in Scotland. The first would be decked in ribbon and lace, and the second as an old wife in a skirt, shawl and ragged hood. She was regarded as unlucky and feared, and was given to a farmer who was late with his harvest. But the bride, as she was also called, was carried from the harvest in triumph, often by the youngest or prettiest girl in the field and hung up above the chimneypiece in the farmhouse.

'Crying the kirn' and 'Cutting the hare' can be likened to the same ceremonies in England, only substituting 'neck' for 'kirn' and 'mare' for 'hare'.

The cailleagh or corn mother sometimes had another part to play. She would, at times, have a large pocket in her old apron, crammed full of bread and cheese, and a sickle stuck in her waistband at the back. With these additions she was welcomed at the harvest supper with a toast from the workers, 'Here's to the one who helped with the harvest'. If there was a dance, she was the first to get a partner.

The accounts from Ireland are mainly not of harvest but of the Eve of Candlemas, the beginning of the farmer's year. This was for many Irish families the signal to sit down and make crosses in rush and straw for the first of February, in honour of St Brigit, a fifth-century Christian saint, who is supposed to have taken over the attributes of Bright, the goddess of fire. Up to the middle of the nineteenth century, simple ceremonies were carried out in the home and the crosses were made to avert evil befalling man or beast.

The National Museum of Ireland has many examples of straw crosses. The majority of them are built up in the medallion form, but there are some plaited with a cross in a circle and others in the form of three-legged crosses that were taken

to hang in the byre and four-legged ones which were put in the house after being blessed.

As in Scotland, the corn mother was called 'cailleagh' and ceremonies much like those in Britain were carried out at harvest time. Harvest knots, in certain areas, were made as part of harvest jollifications. These were decorative knots, made from a single plait and were given as love tokens to the opposite sex. If worn by the girls, the heads of the grain would be kept on, but a twist without heads was customary for the boys.

The last sheaf was preserved in the house or byre until it was replaced by a new sheaf the following year. In some places it was held to possess curative powers and given to sick animals; in others, it was burnt to ashes and made into an ointment to cure skin ailments.

The invention of the threshing machine in 1800 and of the reaper and binding machines in 1881 speeded up the harvest but the

mechanized processes damaged the straw. These modern mechanical aids were instrumental in the decline of corn dolly-making. However, dollies continued to be made in remote places and knowledge of the craft never quite died out. The old plaits were kept alive in the making of harvest crosses in many village churches after the adoption of Harvest Festivals by the Anglican church around 1850.

It was at the Festival of Britain in 1951 that interest was once more aroused in this ancient craft. The festival commissioned Fred Mizen of Essex to make a life-size lion and unicorn in straw. These were much admired and stimulated new interest in the craft. Since then an increasing number of people have been learning the old plaits and making traditional corn dollies.

No craft, however, can remain static and there is a number of plaiters now making new designs and creating beautiful straw work based on the old techniques.

Straw work

The craft of straw work is centuries old. Wherever man has sown cereals, he has harvested not only a staple diet grain but also straw of apparently limited utility. But man's ingenuity over the ages found a variety of uses for this by-product beyond that of animal stabling. Straw was used in brick-making, thatching, cheese preparation, domestic floor covering and in making matting, baskets, fans and many domestic decorative objects.

In warmer climates suitable for palms, the dried fronds were used to make many objects for religious use or personal adornment. Some of the intricate designs and plaits developed in the east were dispersed

70

Preparation for making a 'neck'. The core with five straws tied round it, ready for working. The plait in progress. The completed 'neck' (Top left and right) The five straw close plait, a decorative plait

by sea traders and migrants. Many of them were adapted and used in early western straw work. These designs became traditional and were transmitted through many generations of families. Many regional varieties developed and were also handed down within local families.

Recently there has been revived interest in straw work. A number of craftsmen have mastered old techniques and revived many traditional designs. New designs have also been introduced, using old

techniques based on older designs.

Displays of beautiful examples of elaborate straw work can today be found in many museums, especially collections of traditional corn dollies made by master craftsmen.

Suitable straw

The best straw for making corn dollies is long and flexible, having a well hollowed stalk. In the past, corn yielding straw with these characteristics was popular. But this has been overtaken by the modern trend to produce short, stout stalks with not much cavity.

Straw still varies enormously in size and flexibility according to soil and climatic conditions. Various combinations of these elements can produce vastly contrasting results in different regions, or even localities.

The best time to cut straw for corn dollies is a fortnight before the farmer plans to harvest the crop. The ears should still be upright, and the corn should just be starting to change colour from green to gold. When cut on the turn, the grain should not fall out of the ear in working the straw. Most farmers will be happy to sell or give a sheaf of corn and most will probably take an interest in your project. You need a sickle or clippers to cut the corn 15-20 cm (6-8 in) from the ground. The cut corn then needs to be spread out on a tarpauling and dried in the sun for two or three days. It can then be tied, hung up and stored away from mice and birds.

Corn cut from the field for immediate use requires no preparation other than merely cutting at the first joint and stripping off the leaf sheaf.

Corn that has been stored should be soaked in cold water for about an hour. Older straw from a previous year will require longer. It should then be wrapped in a cloth. It is advisable to dampen only the quantity that you will need for immediate use.

The vast majority of corn dollies are made from hollow or cavity wheat. The old varieties of wheat are becoming difficult to find, but experiments can be made with all types of corn, bearing in mind that corn with a large cavity is required for straw work involving joins. These can be made by cutting off the head of the new straw and inserting the severed end into the hollow in the old straw.

The best straw for making corn dollies is generally taken from such varieties as Maris Widgeon, Maris Ranger, Dove, Eclipse, Elite Lepeuple, Flamingo and Square Head Master. These are all wheat, but corn dollies can also be made of straw from oats, rye, barley and black-bearded wheat, which is imported from Italy and Africa. The

names of farmers and importers who supply straw are listed at the end.

Spirals

Many corn dollies were made with the five-straw spiral plait. This is a plait that was used all over England, right across Europe as far as Turkey and Afghanistan. The same method can be employed with a greater or smaller number of straws and also for plaiting rushes.

The kink made by bending each straw in turn round a prepared core, while it is gently rotated, is most successfully held by wheat straw. Umbrellas, walking sticks and crooks are also made by this method over a suitably shaped core or form.

Neck or sheaf

You will need for all straw work, a pair of sharp scissors and button thread for tying. To make a 30-cm (12-in) neck using the five-straw

1-7 Neck, spiral with core

spiral plait, have ready a good quantity of medium straws, dampened and cut at the first joint with the heads on. Prepare also approximately 12-14 lengths of 18-cm (7-in) and 12·5-cm (5-in) straws cut from below the first joint.

1 Tie seven straws together tightly just above the heads (figure 1).

2 Apply a first layer of the short, headless lengths round the seven straws and tie securely. Do the same with the remaining lengths to form a graduated core swelling out in the middle and tapering off at the top and bottom. Cut the ends of the straws diagonally, leaving one straw uncut at the top (figure 2).

3 Tie the five working straws tightly to the core and spread them out. You may care to practise this part on a dowel beforehand. A and B lie in front of the worker and the heads face downwards (figure 3).

4 Holding the core between thumb and first finger of the left hand, pass A over B and C with thumb and first finger of the right hand. Keep close to the core, bending the straw right over. While in this position give a quarter turn clockwise (figure 4).

5 Pass C over A and D, giving a quarter turn clockwise. Repeat these movements rhythmically with D and E (figure 5).

Joining

After working the five straws for a few rounds, it is essential to join, before the straws become large and stiff. In the best work it should not be possible to detect the joins. They should be distributed throughout the work and not done all at once.

6 Cut the old straw off on a line with the square made by the plait, remove the head of the new straw diagonally and insert into the cavity of the old straw. The succeeding rounds should cover the join completely (figure 6).

7 Carry on working and joining and covering the core. As the plait approaches the top, it gets smaller and smaller, following the shape of the core, until it completely covers the one straw left and becomes the close five straw plait (figure 7). This is bent over to form a loop and attached to the upper part of the neck. A small decorative plait is usually placed over this and an optional bow of ribbon.

Spiral without core: lantern

Lanterns can be made with five, six, seven or nine straws, and they can have two or three smaller lanterns, made with continuous plaiting, at the top, and four other decorative lanterns hanging round the base, often representing the different crops grown on the farm.

In earlier times they were a resting place, in tangible form, of the spirit of the corn, but when all knowledge of their history had been forgotten, they became a little 'cage' as an 84-year-old farmworker from Yockleton, Shropshire, described them, when each year he presented one to his employers for luck.

To make a two- or three-tier lantern, good material is essential.

To make a lantern in five-straw spiral plait

Have ready a quantity of medium straws. Select five straws and tie tightly just below the heads.

8-12 Lantern, spiral without core

1 Spread out the straws and pass A over B and C, making the quarter turn clockwise, exactly as figure 7 was worked for the top of the neck. Work round once, using all five straws (figure 8).

2 Pass A *under* B and C. Turn the work *anticlockwise*. Work all straws in the same way, but bring straw B down alongside, instead of under the last straw. In this position, give the work a quarter turn (figure 9).

3 Two straws lie parallel and facing to the right. Take the lower one and wind round the upper one preserving the square and making the turn *anticlockwise*, working each straw to make the widening square. Keep the work flat and move the left hand to the next position at each turn (figure 10).

4 When the lantern base is the desired size, take the working straw under instead of alongside the next

Celebration crown, an example of the five-straw spiral plait with trefoils in triangular four-plait and bosses in rope plait

straw and back parallel with this straw as in figure 11. The turn should now return to clockwise.

5 Figure 12 shows the square made by placing each straw just inside the square and continuing to turn. Joining should be made at intervals as in figure 6 of the neck, and the finish is also the same as in figure 7.

Two- or three-tier lanterns

Having completed one lantern, extend the close five-plait and build the second lantern on this.

Follow figures 9, 10, 11 and 12 and be sure to have enough length of straw from the close five-plait to make the small platform of the second lantern before joining.

Continue with the same method for the third lantern.

Celebration crown

The straw crown design is known in both the UK and Poland, where it is made at harvest time and presented by the workers to their employers. The Museum of Rural Life at Reading has a straw crown.

An example of the celebration crown was made in 1976 for the Silver Jubilee of Queen Elizabeth II. It was taken out to Busch Gardens, Williamsburg, Virginia, USA for exhibition. A second crown can be seen at Eye Manor, Herefordshire.

How to make a celebration crown

This is a large item as these measurements show:

Height overall: 43 cm (17 in)
Width at widest part: 61 cm (24 in)

73

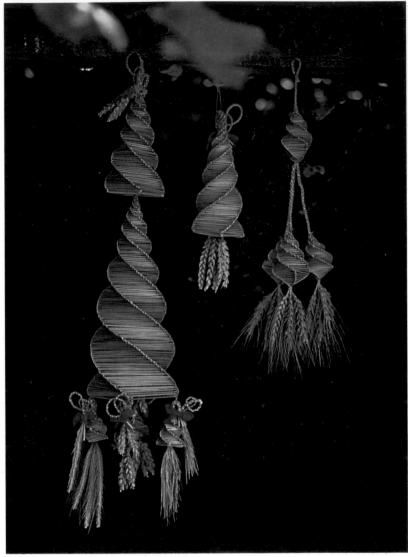

Width at base: 40·5 cm (16 in) two sections

Length of centre pillar to base of crown: 33 cm (13 in)

Length of curved central pillars, each: 36 cm (14 in)

Bosses width: 6·25 cm (2½ in)

length: 91·5 cm (1 yd) of rope plait (see figures 13, 4).

Trefoils in triangular four-plait, each, with a lighter weight wire 51 cm (20 in). The outside edges of the crown are made in two sections. Starting left and right of base and joining at centre top. Each 61 cm (24 in).

The crown is made with the five-straw spiral plait with core (see neck).

Have ready a large quantity of medium and small straws, dampened and cut at the first joint, for working the spiral plait and also a quantity of headless straws (these need not be of such good quality) for padding the core.

Taking careful note of the measurements, cut wires to exact requirements. A 2-mm ($\frac{1}{12}$-in) wire is recommended.

Prepare the shaped cores by slipping a straw over the wire in use (renew as you go on). Pad with suitable lengths of straw for the desired length. Take great care to get the outside shapes graded equally left and right, and the base and centrepieces more heavily padded. On this preparation the final result depends.

(Left to right) A two-tier five-plait spiral without core (lantern); a smaller lantern; the Turkish Kusa Dazi

13–14 Rope plait

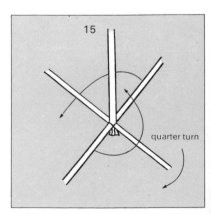

15–16 Triangular four-plait with core

Make all the pieces of the five-straw spiral plait. Tie each firmly, leaving a small piece of wire sticking out (the measurements will allow for this) for ease of assembly.

To make the boss in rope plait

Have ready a small quantity of small straw, dampened and cut at the first joint.

Rope plait

1 Tie six straws tightly together just below the heads (figure 13). Hold with the left thumb and first finger and divide. Twist the upper straws away from you. (Count four to help keep the twists regular.)
2 Bring the twisted straws down over the lower straws. Move the left thumb forward and repeat the twist with what are now the new upper straws. Make sure the plait keeps the same width throughout. The dotted line shows where new straw(s) should be inserted (figure 14). The joins should be anticipated and an old straw discarded after new straw is safely twisted in.

When the length of plait is completed, tie off. Cut off short ends and heads at start of plait. With a needle and button thread, starting in the middle, sew the plait round to form the boss. Make six bosses.

To make the trefoils with triangular four-plait

Have ready the small wire cut to the required length, and a quantity of small straws, dampened and cut at the first joint. Slip a straw over the end of the wire to be used, renew as the work progresses.

Triangular four-plait

1 Select four straws without heads, and tie these round the end of the covered wire (figure 15). Spread them out and work the straws round the wire exactly as for the five straw spiral plait with core, but as only four straws are used, the form of this plait is triangular (figure 16).
2 Care must be taken to keep to

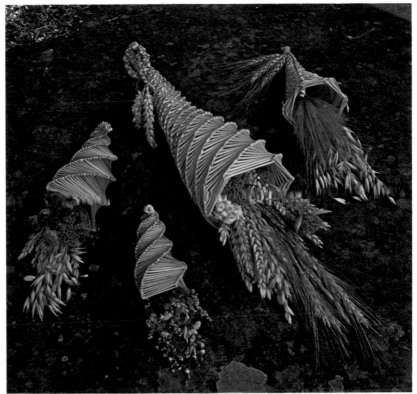

Four cornucopias. The one on the extreme left is made round a wired filling

the same size throughout, approximately 1·4 cm (½ in) for each side of the triangle. Joining is done as in figure 6, spiral with core. Loop into a trefoil shape and tie firmly. Make another. When all parts have been made, study the photograph for assembly. A large needle and button thread was used for most of the ties.

16

Corn dolly design from Guatemala

In this design, reputedly from Guatemala, seven heads of corn are encased in a straw casket, and the suggestion is that they are preserved in this way to secure a good harvest. The idea can be compared to Joseph's dream of seven years of plenty and seven of famine.

To make the Guatemalan corn dolly

Have ready a quantity of large straws dampened and cut at the first joint, with heads.

Select seven straws, tie just below the heads. Instead of letting the heads hang down below, work the spiral plait round the upright heads, gradually expanding and contracting until the heads are covered. At this point start expanding again for approximately five rounds. Attach the last working straw to the next one securely, and cut off close to tie. Bring all remaining straws to a point about 5 cm (2 in) away from the end of the spiral and tie again.

Balances corn dolly in spiral plait

To make the corn dolly
Height from hanger to ends of corn: 18 cm (7 in)
Crosspiece: 7·5 cm (3 in)
Balances each: 2 cm (¾ in) from tie below heads to edge of balance
From edge of balance to crosspiece: 5 cm (2 in)

Have ready a small quantity of very small straws, dampened and cut at the first joint.

The balance
Select five straws with matching heads. Tie just below the heads. Work the five-straw spiral plait for one round and then expand rapidly by placing each straw just outside the straw of the preceding round, for approximately 12 rounds.

Tie off very neatly and finish as for the Guatemalan corn dolly. Make another balance to match.

The crosspiece is worked with the five-straw spiral plait over a very small core (two or three straws). Attach the balances so that they swing a little and hang by a small decorative plait.

Kusa Dazi
This design is from Turkey, and consists of three equal bells. It is best made with a quantity of medium straws, cut at the first joint.

How to make the Kusa Dazi
Overall length: 46 cm (18 in)
Height of each bell: 8·8 cm (3½ in)

Dampen all straws before starting. Tie five straws together under heads. Using the five-straw close plait for one round, expand rapidly by placing each straw just outside the straw of the preceding round. Work only six rounds before decreasing rapidly by bringing the straw just inside the preceding round.

When the bell is complete, leave one straw unworked. Cut to 2·5 cm

(1 in). With remaining four straws, work the four plait as in figure 17 for 10 cm (4 in). Tie off. Repeat for the other two bells.

Tie the three sets of ends of the four-plait together where they finished. Tie five new straws with heads facing upwards round the ends of the plaits. Remove heads and continue as for first bell.

Finish with four-plait (see figure 18). Trim discarded straws to 1·2 cm (½ in).

17 Four plait

18 Kusa Dazi

Cornucopia or the horn of plenty

This design is based on the Greek legend of the origin of the horn of plenty and its associated fertility properties. In Greek mythology Amalthea (who was, variously, the goat that suckled the baby Zeus, or the nymph who reared him or, in one tradition, the daughter of Melissus, king of Crete) brought Zeus up on the milk of a goat. In

19–21 Cornucopia

return Zeus gave Amalthea the horn of the goat, which had the power of giving its possessor whatever he or she wished. This gave rise to the legend of the horn of plenty. This was known to the Romans as the cornucopia.

To make a small cornucopia with a wired filling in the centre

It is 23 cm (9 in) long and 6·4 cm (2½ in) wide at the turn of the spiral.

Select a mixed group of dried flowers, grasses and poppy heads. Tie firmly together. The stalks should be cut to 5 cm (2 in). Hook a 38-cm (15-in) length of green plastic wire through the bunch and secure tightly, leaving the longer end sticking out as in figure 19. Tidy with raffia. Put on one side until cornucopia is made.

Follow the directions for the lantern until stage 5 is reached. At this point make a temporary tie

(Left to right) Scottish doll with a gleaning pocket in her apron filled with heads of oats; doll from Bali; harvest maid; harvest maid with baby; harvest maid on cone, Russian maid

with the working straw and the one next to it, leaving both hands free to cut out the centre and heads. Snip four times, at each corner, to leave a hole 2 cm (¾ in) wide (figure 20). Push the heads and the remains of plait out, and secure all four corners with a needle and thread.

Continue working the spiral, decreasing all the time, until only a small hole is left (figure 21). Pass the wire of the bunch of dried material through the bottom of the spiral until it appears at the top. Work on and round the wire, holding wire securely, for approximately 3·8 cm (1½ in). Cut off the wire. Thread each of the five straws one at a time through the eye of a needle and draw back into the cornucopia. Trim the ends.

77

Harvest maids

In the old days, the making of a harvest maid often consisted merely of tying a bunch of wheat, barley or oats together with a piece of brightly coloured ribbon. With a string to hang her up round her neck, the harvest maid could easily take her place on the wall in either the barn or the kitchen. Sometimes she was a large sheaf of corn wearing baby clothes; at other times, as in Scotland, she could look like a human being in a print dress and white apron with a roomy pocket for gleanings.

Today, the harvest maid will be more durable if she is made round a cardboard cone, so that she can stand. The old cardboard spools from cotton factories are ideal for this use. However, for those who have to make their own, here are instructions for making a card cone.

Cardboard cone

18 cm (7 in) high x 6·5 cm (2½ in) across base.

Prepare a piece of strong brown paper 25 cm (10 in) x 25 cm (10 in). Fold it.

At the top right corner of the folded paper (figure 22) mark 6 mm (¼ in) down, and from this mark 3 cm (1¼ in) across. Cut between these marks. Measure and mark 18 cm (7 in) down fold. From this mark measure and mark 12·5 cm (5 in) across in a straight line to edge of paper.

With a ruler connect A to B. On this line measure and mark 17 cm (6¾ in) from the top. Cut from this mark to the mark on the fold, in a shallow half circle. Open out the pattern and put on lightweight cardboard (shirt-box cardboard is ideal) and cut round. Secure with paperclips top and bottom, adjust-

ing the base width. Glue between paperclips. When ready, remove clips and glue top and bottom.

To make a harvest maid

Height: 46 cm (18 in)

The harvest maid is built up on a 18-cm (7-in) cone. Have ready approximately 52 mixed straws with heads, wheat, oats, black-bearded wheat or grasses. All these will be used dry, and cut at the first joint. Arms are made with 12 damp straws, 30·5 cm (12 in) long.

Pass a fine wire through one of them. Tie together in the middle and at elbows and wrists. Leave under a damp cloth. For the rope plaits that go over her shoulders you will need 12 damp straws with heads, six for one plait and six for the other. Tie six straws together at varying heights, the one furthest from the tie, about 5 cm (2 in). Repeat with the other six straws to match. (See celebration crown for rope plait.)

There is no need to join, as both plaits need only be 6·5 cm (2½ in) long. When finished, tie off, but do not cut off ends of stalks. Keep damp while assembling maid. Tie the 52 dry straws together just under the heads and again 2 cm (½ in) down for her neck.

Open up the body from the side and insert arms. Tie again tightly under the arms.

Cover the cone with adhesive and quickly push up as far as the last tie.

Arrange the straws equally round the cone (an elastic band helps to keep them in place). If there are any gaps push up a headless dry straw. Trim the straws to the edge of cone.

Leave until the straws have adhered, and then start to make the

78

decorative plait that goes round her skirt. If you wish, a simple straw hair plait can take the place of this plait.

Tyrolean plait

This is a flat plait that depends for its effect on folding and flattening the straws at the correct angle. Figures 23 and 24 set up the plait. Figures 25, 26 and 27 show the movements, alternating right and left throughout the plait. Figure 27 shows the plait continuing.

It is best made in oats, although wheat can be used if oats are difficult to obtain.

Have ready a small quantity of dampened oat straws, cut at the first joint, with the heads removed. This plait has been used here as a decorative finish to the skirt of the maid.

It will be necessary to make 27 cm (10½ in) of plait, and this means the plait will have to have new straws inserted. As both ends of the straws are used, this is best done by slipping the larger ends of the new straws over the lips and *vice versa* as the straws run out.

Pull the arms of the maid into shape and tie at the wrists. Arrange the two rope plaits, one at a time over her shoulders, the heads to the front and hanging down her skirt. Tie all the ties round her waist.

Glue the Tyrolean plait in position 1·2 cm (½ in) from the bottom of the skirt. Arrange a small sheaf of mixed dried flowers and corn and attach to one side of the maiden's arms. Finally tie a ribbon bow at her waist.

The Ankh

This is an interesting design based on an early example of the Christian ansated cross, derived from the Egyptian Ankh (see small bride).

To make the Ankh
Height overall: 19 cm (7½ in)
Width of crosspiece: 7·5 cm (3 in)
Inset cross: 5 cm (2 in) x 7·5 cm (3 in)

The Ankh consists of two six-

plaits with core, 23 cm (9 in) long.

The inset cross is made of oats with a fine wire passed through each straw. Have ready 14 large straws of a good length with matched heads, dampened and cut at the first joint.

Six-plait with core
Select seven straws, push a fine wire down one of them right to the head. Tie the remaining six straws round the wired one which is the core (figure 28). Arrange the straws, three on one side and three on the other side of the core. Fold straw A across the front and away behind the back of the core to lie to the right (figure 29). Fold straw B behind and across the front of the core to lie to the left (figure 30).

Work from right to left and take the lowest straw in each case, repeat these two movements for the desired length.

The crosspiece
Cut three large oat straws to the required length. Pass a fine wire through all of them (a drop of adhesive will stop them falling out). Dishcloth cotton can be used for the pairing.

Pairing
Centre the material used: thread, cotton, soft embroidery. Weave first one thread then the other over and under the three oat straws. Tie at the bottom. Do this twice more (figure 31).

The cross
Slip two oat straws over the previously measured wire. Tie firmly with a scaffold knot, the horizontal over the perpendicular.

Assembly
Loop both six-plaits with core and tie them together at butts and tips, one within the other. Flatten them

22 Cone

23–27 Harvest maid, Tyrolean plait

out. Insert the cross; the wire should be just long enough to pierce the plaits. Glue if unsteady. Attach the crosspiece with needle and thread. Arrange one set of heads to advantage. Cut off the other set.

Small bride

This is a half-size version of the large bride of the corn from Fez, Morocco, brought back to England for the first time by Philla Davis in 1969. The shape is similar to the Egyptian symbol of eternal life, the Ankh, which is the Egyptian hieroglyph for life, and consists of a loop over a T. In paintings in the pyramids, the god Osiris is depicted presenting this symbol to Pharaoh and his wife, often held by a loop the other way up. Its appearance in the painting would mean they had

28-30 Ankh, six-plait with core

31 Pairing

32 Small bride, central arm

33 Small bride, right arm

34 Small bride, assembly

Marches fan, an original design by Joan Bourne

already put off mortality and entered on the life to come.

To make the small bride
Height: 33 cm (13 in)
Width: across centre at the widest point excluding heads: 10 cm (4 in)

The design consists of a central arm 10 cm (4 in) from below the heads to the end of the plait.

Four side arms each 12·5 cm (5 in) from below the heads to the end of the plait. Have ready 52 small straws with matching heads of black-bearded wheat, dampened and cut at the first joint.

To make the central arm
Select 12 straws. Tie two together just under the heads. Lay the head of the next straw across these two straws and lying to the left. Bring the stalk round the back of the two straws and finally forward and down to hold the head in position.

Working alternately left and right follow figure 32. Insert five straws each side. Tie about 2·5 cm (1 in) below.

To make the side arms
The side arms are made with ten straws in each using the same technique, except that two arms have all straws set in on the right (see figure 33) and two have them all on the left.

When both sets of arms and central arm are made, tie both sets of the right and left arms together under the heads. Lay one set down the right side up. Lay the central arm on top of this, and the other set of arms on top of that. Study figure 34 for the position of the top straws in the central arm.

Tie both sets of arms together at the top (not including the central arm, which must lie just between).

Tie a temporary tie at the handle end to hold the straws in position. Roughly trim all straws for easier handling.

Spread the arms with a small piece of wood, 5·7 cm (2¼ in) long, and tie the upper and lower sets of arms together between straw 3 and straw 4 of the central arm.

Finally, tie where all arms meet and again at the bottom. Cover ties with raffia to neaten. Leave to dry with the wood stretcher in position, under a weight.

Marches fan
Overall length: 25·4 cm (10 in). 164 straws for the arms of the fan, with heads, approximately 16 headless straws for medallion. A large quantity of straws for the triangular four-plait. Dampen all straws first.

This design is best made with fine small-headed wheat. It is a new design using old techniques.

To make the medallion
Final size: 12 cm (4½ in) x 8·5 cm (3⅜ in).

Prepare a cross of strong wire 12·5 cm (5 in) x 15 cm (6 in). Slip over each wire a large wheat stalk. Tie to form a cross at the centre (horizontal over perpendicular) and with approximately 16 headless straws. Follow instructions for medallion.

This medallion is diamond-shaped, rather than square. The shape is best achieved by slightly overlapping the straws on the horizontal turns.

The medallion is known throughout the world and is sometimes referred to as 'god's eye' and

the winding done in wool or some flexible material.

Holding the working straw in position, along the horizontal cross-bar, wind over and round, rotating the cross, to the next upright. Continue until the straw is used up (figure 35).

Cut the old straw as indicated and put the new straw into the old cavity (figure 36). Continue rotating the cross, and winding. Care must be taken that every join is covered by the succeeding round. Finish by tucking the last straw, suitably trimmed, underneath a straw of the previous round. Do not trim wire until assembly.

To make the right arm
Select 82 straws with matching heads. Tie two straws together as in figure 37; this forms the core. Lay two straws (do not tie) with heads to the right across the core. Carry the stalks round the back of the core and just in front of the heads of the straws. Pull firmly to lock them in position. Select two more straws and continue locking in the same way. Check all the time with the shape of the medallion. It should take 20 locks to get to the crossbar and 20 more to the handle. To secure the free end of the last straws, wind round twice and tuck into centre.

To make the left arm
Select 82 straws and reverse the procedure. To assemble, take the

35–36 Marches fan, medallion

Badsey's fountain, ankh and amulet

The New World cross is a modern design making use of old plaiting techniques, seen in the two Mexican fans called Heart of the Corn at the top and bottom of the cross, and an Irish woven cross behind the central straw rose

two arms and tie them together under the heads. Lay the medallion down, right side uppermost, and over this lay the two arms. Secure the arms at the top to the perpendicular wire of the medallion.

Coax the arms into the shape of the medallion and allow the horizontal crossbar to penetrate the arms at the twentieth lock. Trim the wire if necessary.

Bring the arms together at the base to make a handle, incorporating the extended medallion wire. Tie the handle very firmly at this point and tie again lower down. Trim the handle to approximately 7.5 cm (3 in).

To make the triangular four-plait with core

From the large quantity of straws select five straws and pass a fine wire through one of them. Tie the remaining four straws round the wired straw which is the core (see celebration crown). Work these four straws as for the five-plait spiral with core, joining frequently at the corners to keep the size even. Work enough plait to cover two sides of the medallion, approximately 15 cm (6 in). Repeat for the other side. Tie together under the heads and again at the top of fan. Ease the plaits into position and tie a temporary tie round the handle. With a needle and button thread, secure these plaits invisibly at the crossbar.

To make a three-plait (cat foot)

This plait is a folded plait. It is important to preserve the Y shape throughout, and make the plait at the angle in figure 42.

Select three straws, dampened and cut at the first joint. Tie just under the heads securely. Cut the heads off. (When using this plait for the top of a neck or similar purpose, keep the heads on.)
1 Fold A alongside B (figure 38).
2 Fold B back over A (figure 39).
3 Fold C up and alongside A (figure 40).
4 Fold A sharply down (figure 41).

These four movements are repeated throughout. Figure 42 shows the plait in progress.

The amulet

This is a new design incorporating two traditional (21) group-linked plaits. There is a small lantern in the middle. Rye or wheat can be used.

To make the amulet

Height: 25 cm (10 in)
Width at plait ties: 12 cm (4½ in)

Have ready for the group-linked plaits, 42 straws of rye, with matched heads and stalks as long as

37 Marches fan, right hand

38

A

B

C

38–42 Marches fan, three-plait catfoot

39

A

B

C

84

possible. It is not advisable to join this plait. The plaits should measure 23 cm (9 in) each. Dampen and cut at the first joint. This is not an easy plait and a practice length is advised.

Group-linked plait

Tie the 21 straws together for the first plait just below the heads. Spread them out into four groups of five in each, and one worker. The work should be rotated anticlockwise so that each movement may be made in the same relative pattern towards the worker, clockwise.

When working the plait it will be found that the lowest straw is the one that is used for the next movement. When the plait has advanced a little the straws will automatically fall into place.

Figure 43 shows the grouping of the straws and the first movement. With the right hand, bring A down across groups 1 and 2 over ten straws. Hold A in position with the left hand, count back five straws (ignoring A). Pick up B, the fifth straw in group 2, with right first finger underneath and thumb on top. Secure A also with the right thumb, releasing the left hand to grasp group 4. Give the work a quarter turn anticlockwise, and bring B over groups 2 and 3 into the gap between the groups at the same time. Repeat the whole movement. Make another plait.

Figure 44 shows the plait in progress.

The lantern

This is a small lantern in five-straw spiral plait (see spiral without core). Have ready a quantity of small straws, dampened and cut at the first joint. It is 10 cm (4 in) long excluding the heads to which the plaits are joined, and 2·5 cm (1 in) at the turn of the spiral. At the 10-cm (4-in) measurement, tie the plait together. Cut off one straw and using the remaining four straws, divide and make two plaits 7·5 cm (3 in) long. Loop and tie at the point where the two plaits started.
86

Assembly

Twist the large plaits and tie butts with tips. Push the lantern plaits up between the large plaits and sew securely. Attach a thread hanger unobtrusively behind.

Badsey's fountain

Arthur 'Badsey' Davis, so called because he came from Badsey in Worcestershire, was a great master of the group-linked plait. He used to demonstrate this plait with 49 straws, which was no mean achievement. He copied his father making straw plaits, and taught the skill to his son and his grandchildren. An example of this design can be seen at the Museum of Rural Life, Reading.

To make the fountain

Height: 35·5 cm (14 in)
Width: approximately 15 cm (6 in) across upper plaits, 12·5 cm (5 in) across lower plaits

Have ready a quantity of medium wheat or rye straws with good heads, dampened and cut at the first joint. The dolly consists of one (21) group-linked plait divided off into three (7) plaits, and five close (5) plaits.

43–44 *Amulet, group-linked plait*

Group-linked plait

Select 21 straws with matched heads and of a fair and equal length. Tie together tightly below the heads. Follow the instructions and figures of the group-linked plait (see amulet) and make 5 cm (2 in) of plait. The next step is to divide the 21 straws into three groups of seven straws each and to tie each separately. Two should face to the sides and one up centre back (figure 45).

To make the seven-plait

This is a folded plait and does not rotate. Spread out the seven straws of the first plait over your right hand, holding the rest of the plait between your first and second fingers. Fold with the left hand and hold the straws in position, as they come over with the right or left thumb, where the plait allows it (figure 46).

Fold A down over B and C to lie between C and D. Always work in a clockwise direction. Miss out the next straw D. Fold E over F and G to lie in the gap where A was (figure 47).

Miss out the next straw B. Fold C over A and D into the gap where E was. Continue missing one and folding over two straws until the plait measures 14 cm (5½ in). Tie off. Make two more plaits. When completed, bend two of the plaits down to form a heart shape and tie at start of group-linked plait. Leave the third plait facing up centre back.

To make the close five-plait

Select five straws with heads and tie together under the heads. Work the straws as in figure 7 (spiral with core), making the close five-plait. Make four more plaits. Two of the plaits should be 15 cm (6 in) long, three of them 12.5 cm (5 in) long.

Assembly

Tie two of the longer five-plaits at the head. Tie to the butts of two of the shorter ones, so that the longer ones loop up over the shorter ones. Tie the opposite ends in twos.

Attach the group of plaits 5 cm (2 in) up the centre seven-plait so that the heads lie over the (21) group-linked plait. Tie the other ends two to one side, two to the other, of the heart-shaped seven-plaits.

Tie the last of the shorter five-plaits with heads forward, in a loop at the top of the centre seven-plait.

Harvest supper and festival

The gathering in of crops was the positive result of all the year's work and from the earliest times this has been a season for rejoicing in country districts.

Returning from the last day of the harvest, many workers sang traditional rhymes or snatches of song such as this one from Scotland.

'Baraar's corn's wheel shorn
Bless the day that he was born
Kirny, kirny, oo!
Kirny, kirny, oo!'

(from F. Marion McNeil's *The Silver Bough*).

The harvest supper, called variously Mell, Kirn or Horkey Supper, was held in a barn or, in small communities, in the farmer's kitchen. It was also traditional that the farmer and his wife should wait on the workers. The corn dolly, neck or maiden, whatever shape she might have taken, was hung up in a prominent place and a seat of honour was reserved for the man who had woven the straw and for the girl who had carried it home, and in some cases dressed it.

Harvest suppers are still eaten in many villages, although they are only a shadow of the big suppers, trials of strength, dancing and drinking that used to go on at harvest homes.

In some places, as time went on, money was collected by the head worker, Lord of the Harvest or Horkey Lord, to provide for extra drink at harvest time. This custom was called 'crying' or 'hallowing largesse'. It became much abused and led to excessive drinking and fighting, so much so that in 1850 it was decided to withhold the money levied from all and sundry, and instead to have a large supper to which the whole parish would be invited. This supper would be paid for jointly by the farmers and tradesmen and would be preceded by a church service.

It is this church service that became established as our present

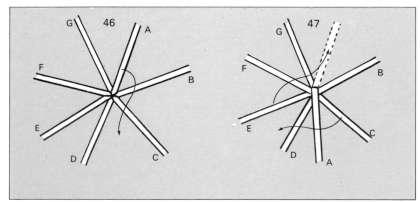

45–47 Badsey's fountain, seven-plait arising out of 21 group-linked plait

Harvest Festival from the 1850s onwards. The idea of bringing harvest produce in the form of corn, fruit, flowers and vegetables to the village church soon became popular. The old traditional corn dolly-makers continued to exercise their skills by making harvest crosses to be taken to the church as a symbol of the corn. In this way the age-old plaits and the pagan corn maiden were preserved. However, the corn maiden was not always welcome. She was treated with suspicion by the Greek Orthodox Church and was not allowed beyond the porches of its church buildings. But intricate straw work is still often found around figures of the Virgin in the rural areas of many Roman Catholic countries.

The old plaiters, in making new corn dollies to be taken to church, succeeded in converting the pagan corn maiden to Christianity. Harvest crosses are still being made and the following is an example of a modern one.

New World cross

The New World cross incorporates two religious hangings from Mexico, a woven cross from Ireland and a design called a straw rose. It is an example of modern work using traditional plaits.

You will require a lampshade ring, 40·5 cm (16 in) across, gilded or bound with raffia. The cross measures 71 cm (28 in) x 48 cm

(19 in). It consists of 25 straws each way using the whole length stripped, without heads. Tie together 5 cm (2 in) from the ends and form a cross, horizontal over perpendicular, at the centre. Have ready a quantity of medium dampened straws and make 2·74 m (3 yd) hair plait.

Hair plait

Tie six medium straws together under the heads, work for 15 cm (6 in), then add and discard as in figure 48 keeping to a width of 5 mm ($\frac{2}{10}$ in), trim heads and stalks. Secure firmly to lampshade ring, binding evenly all round. Tie off. Attach ring on top of cross.

Woven cross

To make the woven cross that lies over the centre of the main cross, cut at the first joint, dampen and remove heads of 36 straws. Arrange in untied bundles of six straws, taking care to reverse the middle bundle so that all the butts are not lying at one end. Lay a brick over three bundles as figure 49 and weave the other three bundles under and over. Move brick, see figure 50, and tie the four bundles in a cross shape very tightly with a clove hitch. Trim to 30·5 cm (12 in) and attach to cross centre.

Heart of the corn

To make the two hearts of the corn, prepare by cutting at the first joint and dampening 40 black-bearded wheat straws (ordinary wheat can

be used if you cannot obtain the black-bearded variety). Grade into two bundles of 20 each, from large to small, bearing in mind that the two hearts should match each other as closely as possible. An important point to remember is that the entire design is turned over after each new straw is laid down and secured. Lay out the first 20 straws of the graded wheat on a working surface. Arrange them in twos according to size (two largest, two not so large) start with the largest and follow in sequence.

1 Lay straw A over straw B. Do not tie. The crossover should be 5 cm (2 in) from under the heads. Holding securely, lay straw C alongside straw A (figure 51).

2 Bend stalk of straw C back and under straw B, over straw A to lie alongside the head of straw B. Holding carefully *turn the whole design over* keeping the heads upright and preserving the diagonal shape (figure 52).

3 Lay a new straw alongside straw B and continue as figure 53. Lock into position by bringing down straw C.

4 New straw is laid down on right. Repeat whole sequence until all straws have been used (figure 54).

To complete, tuck the ends of the last straws under the last loops, back and front. Make another heart of the corn and while still damp lay the hearts down facing each other on the cross, leaving 13 cm (5 in) between them in the centre. Secure

48 *New World cross, hair plait*

49–50 *Woven cross*

with two long pins until the position is adjusted.

Weave the ends of the hearts under and over opposite numbers (they will fall into groups of 3, 4, 3). Tie the last two groups from the top and bottom hearts together and secure to the horizontal bar of the cross. Trim the ends of the hearts. If this design is used as a single item, a hanger can be made, using the top straws on either side.

Straw rose

Have ready a quantity of small wheat dampened and cut at the first joint. Make a hair plait (see New World cross), keeping to the 5-mm (⅕-in) width for approximately 1 m (38 in). Tie off.
1 Hold plait as indicated between left finger and thumb, making a loop about 5 cm (2 in) in depth (figure 55).
2 Working with the right hand and keeping hold all the time of the start of the plait, with the left hand

make four more similar loops (figure 56). There are six loops altogether.
3 Still holding the starting loop, make the last and sixth loop by taking the working end of the plait under the start, over and into the first loop, over and into the fifth and join with the start (figure 57).
4 Completed straw rose. Press together to form a boss and attach to centre of cross (figure 58).

Straw marquetry

It is thought that straw marquetry was first practised in the East and that examples were brought to England in the seventeenth century.

There are accounts of nuns in French and Swiss convents making 'fans, shuttles, sacs and screens' covered by straw marquetry.

The best work was made by prisoners of war from the Napoleonic wars and ranged from miniature chests of drawers to bottles

and work boxes inset with intricate designs in straw. Dartmoor was built for these French prisoners and there were special prisons in many counties, but the most famous for straw work was at Norman Cross, Huntingdon. The best materials are the lower joints of oats, rye, wheat and some grasses, such as cocksfoot or false oats. There are at least six different methods of decorating with straw, all called straw marquetry. The following designs are a mixture of marquetry and straw mosaics.

Preparation

The nodes or knots should be cut out and the pieces of straw soaked for an hour in hot water. They are then split with a knife or thumb nail and ironed flat with a hot iron. The grain of old straw is sometimes coarse. Where this is the case, pass a blunt knife several times over the back of the straw to make it thinner.

Straw marquetry gets its effect by the way the straw is laid. It has a natural shine which does not deteriorate with age.

Straw marquetry ivy leaf

Experiment with material prepared as above. Draw an ivy leaf on a doubled piece of brown paper—a real leaf will do as a pattern—and put one piece on one side. Make a central vein by drawing a line through the centre of the leaf (figure 59). Cut on this line and and apply the prepared straws at an angle, one piece fitting close against the other all up one side of the severed leaf (figure 60). When dry, cut to fit the paper edge. Repeat at a contrasting angle on the other piece of the severed leaf (figure 61). When both are covered, fit together first one side and glue, then glue the other side to the original uncut leaf shape. This can be used stuck to coloured felt as a paperweight. The same method can be used to make a marquetry picture such as the sea horse described here (figure 62).

51–54 Heart of the corn

Marquetry sea horse

Have ready a quantity of prepared oat straws (see preparation for straw marquetry). Trace the design on to a doubled piece of brown paper (figure 62). Cut out the whole design. Put the plain pattern on one side. Cut out the marked areas on the design pattern very carefully, noting the position of one piece with the next. Cover with straw as with ivy leaf. The hatching on the pattern shows the correct angles to apply the straw. Trim straws to brown paper shapes. When all the pieces of the design have been covered and trimmed, stick carefully on to the plain brown paper pattern, fitting the whole design together. Trim if necessary. The snail, shell and leaves are made this way.

The seven circles are superimposed. Use a compass, or correct-sized button or punch to make them. Glue to the design, the largest for the eye.

Stick the sea horse to a felt covered piece of card 18 cm (7 in) x 23 cm (9 in) and complete by gluing this to a contrasting card.

Marquetry cockerel

This cockerel was made partly in natural and partly in coloured straws. These are not always easily available, but can be obtained at some craft shops at Christmas-time.

The making of the cockerel does not differ from the sea horse except in one respect. After tracing the whole design and cutting out, make a separate tracing of the centre wing and headpiece (figure 63). The wing should be superimposed and the headpiece slightly overlapped when the design is being assembled. Feathers and wattles are applied last.

Metal templates for use in patchwork

Small 1·2-cm ($\frac{1}{2}$-in) diamond templates can be used for geometrical designs. These have the advantage of fitting together accurately. Boxes can be covered in this way. It is a good thing to plan out the proposed design beforehand, taking into consideration the size of the box. Brown dyed straws were employed as a contrast in the following design.

Marquetry box

To cover a box 8 cm ($3\frac{1}{10}$ in) x 8 cm ($3\frac{1}{10}$ in) x 3·5 cm ($1\frac{2}{5}$ in). You will require: a hexagon set of

55–58 Straw rose

59–61 Ivy leaf

*62 Pattern for straw marquetry sea
horse*

1·2-cm (½-in) patchwork templates, graph paper, prepared straws (soaked, split, flattened and ironed) natural and dyed as desired, and a pair of sharp scissors.

Draw a horizontal line and a perpendicular line crossing in the centre of the box lid. From the graph paper cut out the exact size of the lid. Draw lines to correspond with those on the lid.

Stick some of the prepared straws on to brown paper, close together. Four shapes have been used from the patchwork set—hexagon,

diamond, half hexagon, triangle (figure 64). Starting with the hexagon, place this on the prepared straws on brown paper and cut out the shape precisely. The whole pattern depends on accuracy in cutting.

Continue cutting from the other templates until enough have been cut to start to arrange the pattern. Stick the hexagon in the centre of the graph paper pattern and work outwards, sticking as you go. When the design has been completed, cut four segments from the corners,

marking each one on the back and severing at the crossing lines (see figure 64).

Stick the main design on to the box lid. Cover the severed segments with straws at differing angles all round, doing each one separately for the best results. Trim if necessary. If the box lid is bevelled apply a small straight edging to help in joining to the sides. Cover the sides in the same way with suitable designs for the shape.

Boxes are best preserved with a coat of clear varnish when com-

*Straw marquetry cockerel, built up by
applying straws at contrasting angles
on brown paper patterns. The wing
is added later*

pleted. There are all sorts of patchwork templates that can be used
and shapes can also be cut from
graph paper or accurate line draw-
ings. As experience is gained, work
can be started straight on the box.

Marquetry collage

To make a marquetry collage, a
strong piece of card covered with
felt, hessian or fabric will be needed.
Any leaf shape may be used, but the
collage illustrated is of ferns in
natural oat straws.

Prepare in the same way as for
the ivy leaf (see preparation for
straw marquetry). Note how the
spine of the leaf is drawn to leave the
stalk in one piece (see figure 65).

Before mounting the two halves,
glue a fine wire on the second
template to run along the centre
of the stalk but just off the centre of
the leaf. This gives flexibility to the
leaf and the stalk can be lightly
glued to a piece of old ivy root or

similar material. The small leaf has
straw on the back and front.

Marquetry collage of leaves,
berries tendrils and stars

This is made up on a circle of thin
brown card covered with horizontal strips of natural straw, prepared as for marquetry. A length
of peeled honeysuckle outlines the
circle three times.

64 Marquetry box

To make the leaves, use natural
leaf shapes and prepare as for the
fern collage. To make the tendrils,
take a piece of split flattened straw
3 mm ($\frac{1}{8}$ in) wide, and dampen this
before starting. Have ready a
heated knitting needle. Wind the
straw round this and secure with
adhesive tape. Leave in position for
several minutes and then slip off
the needle. A small, regular spiral
will result.

To make the large star

On a piece of plain or graph paper
draw a 10-cm (4-in) square. Draw
lines down the centre and across
from side to side, also diagonally
from corner to corner (figure 66).

Mark the diagonals at 5 cm (2 in)
from the centre. Mark all lines 2 cm
($\frac{3}{4}$ in) from the centre. Connect the
2-cm ($\frac{3}{4}$-in) marks with the eight
points of the stars. Where the lines
intersect draw lines to the centre.
These shapes are the lozenges,
repeated eight times, that consti-
tute the pattern for the star. Cut
out and cover each with prepared
straw, that has been dampened,
split and ironed, applying the straw
down the lozenge, not across.

To assemble, draw a circle with a compass on brown paper or thin card 2·5 cm (1 in) diameter, and mount the lozenges on this.

The smaller star is made in the same way, with the overall dimensions 7·6 cm (3 in) and an inner radius of 1·2 cm (½ in).

To make a berry or ball

Experiment with paper before attempting in split, flattened and dampened straw. Three strips of paper or straw are needed, each 11·5 cm x 6 mm (4½ x ¼ in).

To facilitate working the straw, draw the back of a knife across the underside of the first two strips.

A square straw marquetry box and ivy-leaf paperweight

Wind the first strip twice round the finger and arrange for the joint just to overlap. Slide off and glue in place, and hold with a paper clip.

Make a second ring in the same manner. When the glue has dried, remove the paper clips and push the first ring inside and at right angles to the second ring. Take the third strip, dampened in the case of straw. Cut at an angle and thread this end under the inner ring, over the outer ring and so on, to form a third interlocking ring. Glue in place. Swivel round to hide joins.

Star from a single strand

This star, as its name implies, consists of a single flat strand which is held in position either by contrary turns or continuous winding laid at specific angles.

It is advisable to practise in firm paper before attempting it in split flattened straw.

Miniature three-point star

Take a single length of split, flattened straw of either oats or rye, 33 cm x 6 mm (13 x ¼ in).

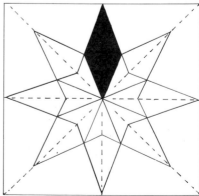

66 Flat star marquetry

65 Fern collage

Re-dampen straw. If it curls, pass over the back of a knife.

1 With the wrong side towards you, cut off the end at 60° (figure 67).

2 Fold up to make an equilateral triangle (figure 68). This is the top side of the star throughout and the work should not be turned over at any time, nor should the triangle be rotated at this stage. This is the foundation of the actual star.

3 Wrap the free end eight times round the original triangle, finishing with the free end coming from under the triangle, lying towards the right (figure 69).

4 Holding the triangle in the left hand, swivel it slightly anticlockwise, so that the point lies on top and in the centre of the free end (figure 70).

5 Wrap the free end round itself once (figure 71).

6 Rotate the triangle anticlockwise, until the next point takes up the same position as before (figure 72).

7 Wrap again (figure 73).

8 Repeat with the third point (figure 74).

9 Continue wrapping each point in turn (figure 75). The points will extend with each round gradually and layers will become apparent towards the centre of the star. Three layers on each point should be sufficient. Finish by tucking the end under the previous straw at the back as shown in figure 76.

Straw marquetry seahorse. The design is built upon brown paper patterns and the straws applied at contrasting angles

Fern collage

94

67-76 Miniature three-point star

Circular collage

Books for further reference

The Craft of Straw Decoration	A. Coker	Dryad Press	1971
Straw Mosaics	Lena Croucher	Dryad Press	
New Golden Dolly	M. Lambeth	Cornucopia Press	1966
Gold Dolly: the Art, Mystery and History of Corn Dollies	M. Lambeth	J. Baker	1969
Straw Craft: More Golden Dollies	M. Lambeth	J. Baker	1974
Straw Work and Corn Dollies	Lettice Sandford	Batsford	1974

Useful addresses

Straw
Bill Armitage West Hall Farm Sedgeford Hunstanton Norfolk
David Butler Woolley Green Farm Braishfield Romsey Hants
G. A. Liddle Foxholes Farm Hanbury Burton-upon-Trent
C. Payne 2 Stoneyrock Cottage Nags Head Lane Great Missenden Bucks

Occasional
Bevin Dairy Farm West End Welford Rugby
Gardner Myton Farm Warwick
Steven Lower Littleton Farm Chew Road Winford Somerset
Trick Fellon Farm Brockham Surrey
W. J. Tucker Trewornan Farm Wadebridge Cornwall

Black-bearded wheat
G. Smalley 1 Pasture Lane Ruddington Nottingham NG11 6AE

Boxes for marquetry
GML Plastics Deritend Birmingham
Hobby Horse 15-17 Langton Street London SW10
Leisure Craft Centre 2-10 Jerdan Place London SW6 5PT

Coloured straws in bulk
Trinkhalm Industrie Pauer & Co. Bremen Germany

Paperweights
H. Thorn & Son 118 Fore Street Exeter EX4 3JQ

Templates
The Needlewoman Regent Street London
JEM Patchwork Templates 18 St Helen's Street Cockermouth Cumbria

Say it with flowers— the personal way

Pressed flowers and dried flowers, either in free-standing or in framed compositions to hang on the wall, make delightful decorative features for any home. Flowercraft needs very little special equipment—simply a little imagination on the part of the creator. Once you have tried it, you will find you have a wonderful means of preserving the memory of a special occasion, such as a wedding, a visit to a particularly lovely place or a bouquet from a friend.

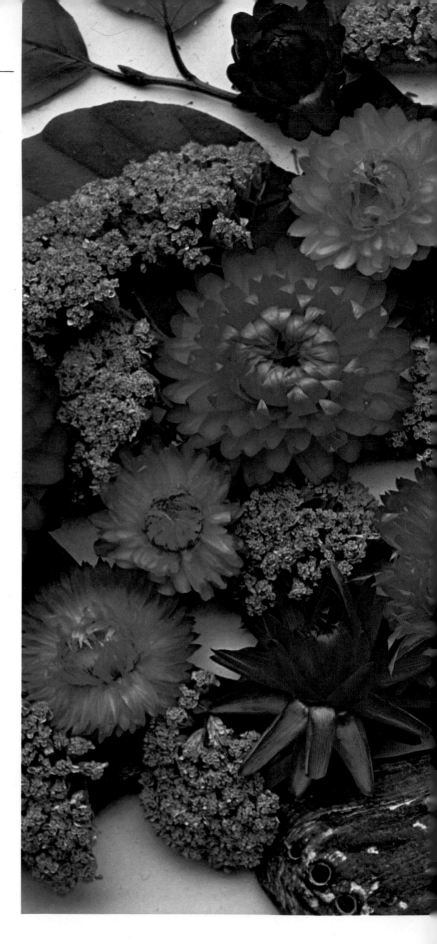

Preserving plant material

Preserving leaves, flowers and grasses gives anyone who wishes the opportunity of brightening their home throughout the year with decorative arrangements made from natural material. But it does much more than this. It can also enable us to capture and preserve special or nostalgic occasions in a unique way. A wedding bouquet can be pressed and kept forever. Leaves and grasses collected on a memorable day in the country can be dried and made into an arrangement which gives them a particular and personal significance. Flowers grown in the garden can be preserved and made into a picture to bring back summer's pleasures in winter.

There is a number of ways of preserving plant material. Scores of plants and grasses can be easily and effortlessly dried. Others can be preserved with the help of glycerine. Many flowers will retain their colour if treated with a desiccant. The method of preservation that you choose will depend on the nature of the material you wish to preserve and how you intend to use it—for example, whether in a picture, for a small or large arrangement, or for a greetings card.

The preservation methods most commonly used are drying, preserving with the use of glycerine or a desiccant, and pressing. Dried plants have been used in arrangements for many years. Such arrangements, however, have mostly consisted of those plants which, given the right weather conditions, dry naturally on the stalk out of doors. Pampas grass, Chinese lanterns, honesty and teasels have been perennial favourites. It is only recently that people have begun to extend their imaginations by experimenting with all types of foliage, flowers and grasses. Today the range of natural materials that can be dried seems almost limitless and

is continually being increased as new things are tried. This has made the variety of possible arrangements much greater and certainly more interesting.

Preserving with glycerine is a more recent craft than that of drying. Glycerine gives a more supple and generally less brittle result, since the glycerine is taken up into the plant and remains in its cells even when the water has evaporated. The natural colour of the plant is changed in the process —it usually turns darker—but the glycerine content gives it a deep sheen or lustre.

Drying with desiccants has become a little less laborious with the introduction of commercial desiccants. Sand has long been used, but it needs a great deal of thorough washing, drying and sifting before it is in a suitable condition for use. This method of drying ensures that flowers retain both their colour and shape. However, they are extremely fragile and will in time re-absorb moisture.

Pressing flowers is an old craft, much practised by the Victorians, who valued their pressed-flower pictures.

Preserved plants can be used in all sorts of ways. For example, in the making of pictures, greetings cards and myriad arrangements using all manner of containers, in paperweights, to decorate waste-paper baskets, lampshades, trays or gift-wrapped presents. Leaves and flowers, either dried or preserved in glycerine, are best for free-standing arrangements. They may vary in size from something to brighten an invalid's meal tray to a large arrangements to fill an empty fireplace. In this way you can enjoy flowers in your home even when fresh ones are prohibitively expensive or despite your lack of success with indoor house plants. In addition, dried flowers are long-lasting and are not affected by central heating, although if you are planning an arrangement for a shelf

above a radiator it is wise not to allow the foliage to come into direct contact with the heat.

Preserved foliage is also invaluable for adding background and for filling out a vase of fresh flowers. Glycerined beech leaves can greatly complement the rich autumnal colours of chrysanthemums. However, since the preserved leaves will have to be put into water with the fresh flowers, it is a good idea to dip the ends in melted candlewax, sealing wax or nail polish to prevent them from rotting.

The key to the creative use of preserved plants is to experiment with preservation methods. Do not imagine that something will not dry or press until you have tried it out. There is an unpredictable element in preservation and you might well be surprised and delighted with the results.

Different methods of preservation
Drying

Drying is the easiest of all methods of preservation. In general, it involves no more than hanging the leaves, flowers, grasses or seedheads upside down in small bunches in an airy place and leaving them to dry. This drying technique is suitable for many garden flowers and grasses, for a wide variety of seedheads and for the group of flowers known as everlasting.

In most cases flowers should be picked when they are dry and just about fully opened (but see list for individual exceptions). Pick them with as long a stalk as possible, but strip the stalk of all its leaves because these do not dry successfully. Tie the flower stems in small bunches—large flowers can be handled singly—and suspend them upside down from a line of string in a dry place. Ideal conditions are a shed or an airing cupboard which is airy and warm, but not too light. Some flowers will fade dramatically if they are subjected

to strong sunlight; others will lose their colour if they dry too slowly.

Grasses should be picked on a sunny day when they are quite dry. This can be any time from early summer to autumn, but for the best results, the ideal time is when the stamens are just beginning to appear. In most cases it is a good idea to strip off the leaves since they do not dry well. If you want firm, rigid stems, tie the grasses in bunches and suspend them upside down from a line in the same way as for flowers. However, if you would like some to bend and droop (perhaps to give softness to the sides of an arrangement), put them vertically in a jug or jar and just leave them to dry.

Grasses are fully dried when all the moisture has gone from their skins. The colour of dried grasses will depend very much on the time and the weather conditions at picking. If there is a very hot spell in early summer, so that you can pick the grasses when they are very young, they will dry to a lovely, fresh green. Picked later in the year, they are more likely to dry to a creamy brown colour.

Many seedheads — poppies, peonies, teasels—will begin to dry while still on the plant. Allow them to dry naturally for a while, but bring them indoors to finish drying since bad weather conditions later in the year might spoil them.

Dried plant material is very fragile and must be stored and handled carefully. Long stems of grasses, flowers and seedheads should be laid carefully in big cardboard boxes and kept in a dry place. Individual flowerheads (helichrysum, for example) can be kept in small boxes, shoe or shirt boxes. When thoroughly dried, put the lid on the box as this helps to keep the bright colours of the flowers.

Suitable flowers, seedheads and grasses

Everlasting flowers

Achillea, yarrow Clusters of little yellow or pink flowers grow on long, strong stems. Pick them just before all the heads have come out and hang up singly, or leave standing in a jar. The stalks are useful as false stems for other flowerheads. Large clusters of flowerheads can be used in an arrangement, or they can be taken apart and used in pictures.

Anaphalis pearl everlasting White flowers with small pale grey leaves. Pick just as the petals open, strip off leaves and hang up in small bunches leaving a short stalk. They do not take long to dry.

Gomphrena Small, round flowerheads in a variety of colours. Hang in bunches in a cool airy place.

Helichrysum, everlasting This is one of the most useful and easy to dry of all everlasting flowers. The small chrysanthemum-type flowers which come in a wide variety of colours from cream, through a range of yellow and orange to deep

scarlet and rust. The stalks do not dry successfully, so pick the flowerheads with a small stalk only and dry them individually in a seed tray or similar container. Drying in the sun does not appear to affect the colours of these flowers. If you want to use them in arrangements you will have to give them false stems.

Helipterum or *Acroclinium* Semidouble daisy-like flowers, that may be pink, white or yellow. Pick before petals are fully opened and hang upside down in a cool airy place. Some will turn green when dried.

Lonas This is sometimes difficult to obtain. It has tiny flowerheads of a lemony-yellow colour, but they can be dyed a variety of colours.

Lunavia, honesty You can pick this throughout the growing period for a variety of effects; picked early when it is green, it will retain the green colour as it dries. If you leave it until it is papery and silver in colour it will already be dry, strip off seed cases and remove seeds. If it is necessary to hang up in bunches do not crowd in too many sprays.

Physalis, Chinese lanterns Pick when the lanterns are orange, which will be during September or October. There is no need to hang them—they will already be dry. Just take off the leaves and put the lanterns into an arrangement.

Rhodanthe The flowers are coneshaped and white to pink in colour, which they retain well as they dry.

Statice There is a variety of differently shaped and coloured everlasting flowers within this group, including pink pokers and sea lavender. Hang up to dry in bunches.

Xeranthemum Purple flowers with strong stems. They hold their colour magnificently as they dry.

Garden flowers

Amaranthus viridis Has long hanging green flowers which turn cream when dried.

Centaurea macrocephela Pick as the central flower is drying. Pull this out, strip off the leaves and hang up the stem and flower bract to dry.

It looks attractive with a helichrysum stuck in the middle.

Delphinium and larkspur Pick before top flowers are out. Hang up singly so as not to crush flowers and dry until papery. They keep their colour very well.

Echinops, globe thistle Pick while the bud still has points, before the flowers open. If you wait until the flowers are out, they will drop off in the drying. Strip all the leaves and hang individually—it has a very firm stalk.

Erica, all heathers Treat in the same way as hydrangea. Lavender pink seems to be the most successful, but try others too. You may find that some flowerheads drop off.

Globe archichoke Pick when the flower is mauve before it is completely open. Hang up individually to dry—the flowerheads will turn cream.

Hydrangea Pick flowers towards the end of September when they are dry and the petals are papery to touch. They are treated in a different way to the other flowers. Cut the stems and stand them in a jar with at least 2·5 cm (1 in) of water. Put in a warm place (such as an airing cupboard) and leave until all the water has been absorbed. Then leave them until flowers feel crisp. If you put them in too hot a place, they may absorb the water too quickly and shrivel.

Limonium There is a number of varieties of this flower, many of which are similar in appearance to statice but are not termed everlasting. Cut stems just before flowering and hang up to dry.

Polygonum affine The small, condensed flowerheads appear in a variety of pinks and reds. Pick when it is flowering, strip off leaves and hang up in bunches. The leaves press very well.

Seedheads

Acanthus, bear's breeches Pick when the flowers, which may be pink, white or mauve, are in bloom

The background for this picture was made of plywood painted with emulsion paint. The frame was homemade. It used a subtle combination of pressed and dried flowers. The shell, chosen for its harmonizing colours, was positioned first to provide the focal point. The top leaves were put in next and the other leaves spaced out to make the outline design. Finally, the helichrysum and seedheads were added to fill in the centre of the design

and hang up individually to dry in a warm place. The tall stems make them useful for large arrangements, but beware of the prickles on the leaves.

Clematis Certain varieties, such as *Clematis tangutica*, produce a round, bright green ball of curled silk seedheads which look lovely in pictures. Pick when the flowers are dead and the seedheads are visible. Hang them up or dry them flat in a box.

Crocosmia, montbretia Dried for the seedhead, you would pick these when the flowers have died. You can also try drying the flowers, in which case you should pick before the top flowers are out, but the flowers may fall out.

Digitalis, foxglove Pick when flowers have gone and hang up individually to dry. Useful for tall arrangements, but the seedpods are also pretty used singly in pictures.

Dipsacus fullonum, teasels Teasel seedpods will dry on the stalk after the lavender blue flowers have gone. Bring them in when they are dry—there is no need to hang them up. An interesting result is obtained if you set fire to the dried heads (do this in the garden) then shake out the fire, so you have an attractive charred head.

Eryngium, sea-holly Pick after flowers have fallen, by which time the stem will be just about dry. The tall sprays are good for large

arrangements. You can also try drying the pale blue flowers, but they often lose their colour.

Iris Beardless iris produces extremely attractive seedpods. Pick when they have gone to seed. They dry to a rich dark brown.

Iris foetidissima This variety has large oval bulbous seedheads, which, depending a little on the weather, may split open in the autumn to reveal little bright orangey red seeds inside. If they do not open by themselves you can squeeze them open. If the seeds fall out, carefully glue them back in again. Alternatively, if you spread glue lightly over the seeds, this will hold them in place.

Molucella laevis, bells of Ireland Pick as the tiny white flowers are falling and remove the leaves. Hang up the long sprays individually to dry until they are papery and a rich creamy colour. You can also preserve them by the glycerine method.

Muscare, grape hyacinth Pick when flowers have died and the seedhead is white (but wait until seeds have fallen).

Nigella, love-in-the-mist The large seedheads vary in colour from cream to purple and look lovely in an arrangement. Leave until the flowers (which may be white or blue) have died. Alternatively, if you pick them when they are still in flower and hang them to dry, they may retain both petals and seedhead intact. This will not always work, though and often the flowers have to be removed.

Onions The large round seedheads are very useful for arrangements, or can be cut in half and used in pictures. If wanted for arrangements, hang up the whole stalk to dry.

Paeonia, peony Leave for a month or so after the flowers have completely died and the seedhead will grow bigger. It is a beautiful shape —like a stag's horn—and it is very soft and velvety.

Poppies Leave until the seedheads appear and all the petals have fallen. Hang up to dry. All types of poppy, wild ones included, are useful.

Staychs lanata, silver carpet or rabbit's ears Pick in late summer when all the flowers have gone. The leaves and seedheads dry well, but need very careful handling as the leaves particularly are very brittle when dried.

Typha latifolia, bullrush Pick in late summer or early autumn, as soon after they have turned brown as possible. If you leave them too long before picking they blow very easily. Spraying with hair lacquer will help to prevent them blowing.

For this picture, an old frame and white-faced hardboard were used as the background. The plant material was beech and laurel leaves that were preserved in glycerine and positioned after the shell, and also small, dried flowerheads of achillea and helichrysum

Table I Plants suitable for natural drying

Border flowers	Everlasting flowers	Grasses
Acanthus	Acrolinium	Hare's tail
Achillea, gold plate	Anaphalis	Pampas
Amaranthus (green variety)	Helichrysum	Pennisetum
Delphinium	Rhodanthe	Quaking
Echinops	Statice (especially Limonium bonduellii)	Sweet corn (after fertilization)
Eryngium		
Golden rod		
Monkshood		
Stachys lanata		

This table of some of the suitable material for drying is by no means comprehensive. A lot of interesting material can be found by trial and error.

Grasses

The instructions given at the beginning of the list apply to all grasses, wild or cultivated. Packets of seed for ornamental grasses are available from seed merchants and will commonly contain the following.

Annual

Briza maxima, quaking grass
Lagurus, hare's tail
Bromus macrostachys
Bromus madritensis
Eragrostis elegans
Pennidryum lonhistylum
Pennisetum ruppellii
Triticum

Perennial

Milium
Molinia
Stipa
Koeleria

Preserving in glycerine

Plants preserved in glycerine are more supple and less fragile than when dried. They last almost indefinitely and may be washed with warm, soapy water if they get dusty or dirty. Glycerine preservation is a suitable method for various types of foliage and the foliage may be gathered over a period of time. The important thing is that the foliage should be picked when it is mature but still taking up sap. If the picking is delayed until the leaves are changing colour and are no longer taking up the sap, they will then be unable to assimilate the glycerine. Equally, if you pick sprays of foliage in which the leaves are still soft and immature, they will tend to go limp quickly, as at this stage they do not easily take up glycerine.

Summer is the best time for picking foliage. Pick throughout these months, since you will get different results from the various stages of maturity. Be sure to select well shaped sprays with leaves that are undamaged. Scrape the bark off woody stems for about 4 cm (1½ in) from the end of the stem and split the ends of hard or thick stems. Other stems should be cut on a slant and any low growing, damaged or unwanted leaves should be removed.

Mix one part glycerine with two parts of hot water in a jar or jug. Cold water will not mix well with glycerine. Do not heat the mixture. The sprays of foliage can be put into the mixture while it is still warm. See that it comes about 5 cm (2 in) up the stem. If the sprays are large and heavy stand the jug in a bucket to avoid the risk of toppling over.

Leave the sprays in the glycerine mixture until all the leaves have turned a uniform colour, which will generally be darker than the original colour, but can vary from beige to almost black. If the sprays take up all the solution before a uniform colour is achieved, add some more solution. Any solution left over can be used again. The length of time taken varies with individual types of foliage, from a few days for laurel to several weeks for box or magnolia.

Better results are sometimes achieved with large, heavily tissued leaves if they are mopped with, or immersed in the glycerine solution, since it can take rather a long time for the stem to take up and absorb the moisture. Mop large leaves on both sides with cotton wool soaked in the solution and then stand the stem in it in the jar. Drop smaller leaves, such as ivy, directly into a dish of the glycerine and water mix. Foliage preserved in glycerine is most useful for combining with fresh flowers since it is not harmed by being placed in water. The preserved foliage should be stored in a dry place when it is not in use,

106

The dramatic red background used here is Dralon. The design was started by fixing down the two shells and the centre point was accurately located for this. The outline was established by the bought bleached ferns (it is best not to bleach your own). These were positioned so that the exterior outline was kept equidistant from either edge. The acuba leaves were put in next and then the centre flower. Finally, the design was built up with flowerheads and naturally bleached seedheads

either hanging in bunches or wrapped in paper. If the foliage is allowed to get damp it will become mildewed.

Suitable foliage

Acuba, spotted laurel This should be picked in summer. *Acuba* takes about three weeks to absorb the glycerine and turns almost jet black, entirely losing its variegated colouring. The leaves are superb for pictures. They will need wiring and a false stem if they are wanted for arrangement since the sprays go very limp.

Aspidistra This takes about twelve weeks for the stems to absorb glycerine completely, but the process can be speeded up if the leaves are mopped as previously instructed. The leaves turn a beige colour.

Beech Pick during the summer. Beech will take from one to two weeks to absorb the glycerine and turns various shades of brown depending on its maturity at the time of picking.

Buxus, box Pick when mature. The tiny leaves will turn brown. The short sprays are useful for small arrangements—they are not flat enough for pictures.

Cotoneaster Make sure all the leaves are fully developed before picking. If they are not mature to the end of the sprig, they will go limp. Pick after the plant has flowered but before the berries appear. *Cotoneaster* takes two to three weeks to absorb the glycerine and the colour will vary according to type.

Eucalyptus Do not pick until the leaves are really mature or they will go limp. They will either turn brown or a lovely silvery-grey in

colour, according to type.

Fatsia If it is stood upright, fatsia can take up to ten weeks to be fully preserved. This can be speeded up by immersing the leaves in the glycerine solution.

Laurus nobilis, common laurel This can be preserved at most times of

107

Table 2 Plants suitable for preservation with glycerine

Foliage	Weeks	Comment
Aspidistre	12	mop, beige
Atriplex	$\frac{1}{2}$	beige
Beech	1–2	green beech more successful
Bergenia	3–4	Immerse
Box	3–4	beige
Broom	2	almost black
Camellia	4	dark brown
Choisya	3	light beige
Cotoneaster	2–4	colour varies with type
Elaeagnus	4–6	variegation is lost
Fatsia	2–6	mop or submerge
Ferns	2	pick when spores show
Grevillea	2	colour varies
Ivy	2–3	mop or submerge
Hellebore	2–3	light brown
Laurel	2–3	very tough, dark brown
Magnolia	3–4	tough, dark brown
Mahonia	2–3	medium brown
Oak	2	light brown
Pittosporum	2	medium brown
Rhododendron	2	single leaves better
Rose	2	use woody stem, dark green
Rubber plant	4	mop or submerge
Solomon's seal	1–2	treat after flowering
Spotted laurel	3	variegation lost, dark brown
Sweet chestnut	1–2	single leaves better
Whitebeam	2	brown with grey underside

Other plant material

	Weeks	Comment
Garrya elliptica catkins	3	treat in spring
Hydrangea flowers	2	use woody stems
Iris seedpods	2	useful shape
Lime flowers	2–3	remove leaves
Old man's beard	2	treat before flowers open
Pussy willow catkins	2	treat when silky
Sea-holly flowers	2–3	light brown
Teasels	3	treat when green

The times given are only a guide. Weather, time of picking and temperature may all affect the process.

the year and is very tough. The leaves turn brown.

Magnolia The leaves turn dark brown after three to four weeks and are very tough.

Mahonia Wait until the leaves are bright green before picking, then they will keep their shine. The leaves are preserved after about three weeks, but they will turn darker if you leave them for longer. The fan-shaped sprays will need wiring if they are to be used in an arrangement, since they tend to go rather limp.

Quercus, oak The stalk can be preserved straight and erect, but the leaves tend to droop. Oak is useful for filling in the sides of arrangements.

Paeonia, peony The leaves turn a dark olive green after two weeks. However, they are very limp and are really only useful for sticking down as a picture background.

Rhododendron Pick the leaves after the flowers have died. After about two to three weeks they will turn a deep brown colour.

Suitable flowers

Clematis vitalba, old man's beard Pick before the flowers open. Separate the stems and strip off the leaves. Leave in a glycerine solution for about two weeks.

Hydrangea Flowers can be treated this way instead of with water alone.

Molucella leavis, bells of Ireland Pick when they have finished flowering and strip off the leaves (which grow right up to the top of the stem). The flower bracts will turn a creamy beige.

Polygonatum, Solomon's seal Pick when the little white flowers have all appeared. Leave in the glycerine solution until the stems have absorbed it all.

Some seedheads can also be glycerined instead of just being left to dry. Those suitable include:

Acer plantanus, sycamore Pick after flowering, when the seed pods are very young.

Dipsacus fullonum, teasels Pick while they are still green.

Drying with desiccants

This is a more laborious method of preservation than the other two methods, although the marketing of commercial desiccants has made it considerably easier than it was in the days when sand was the most common medium. Sand has been used for many years to preserve flowers, but it needs a great deal of preparation since it has to be washed several times, then dried and sifted. Other desiccants used are silica gel, borax and alum.

Silica gel is the quickest, but is also probably the most expensive desiccant to use. If you do not buy it ready ground, crush with a rolling pin until thoroughly powdered. After use it can be dried in a low oven and re-used. Full instructions are given by the manufacturer.

Borax and alum are best mixed together in the ratio of two parts of alum and one part of borax. Borax is very light and this makes it suitable for delicate flowers, but it tends to be rather sticky and does not give sufficient support to the petals.

Most flowers can be preserved by using desiccants, but begin by preserving simple types which have a single ring of petals rather than those of a more complicated construction. The advantage of drying this way is that the colour of the flower is retained. The disadvantage is that the preserved result is very fragile and delicate. The dried flowers will also fade in strong sunlight and will reabsorb moisture.

In this picture the pattern has been balanced and the curve created naturally by the shapes of the material. The bleached fern was positioned first and then the stronger, coloured acuba leaves. The centre was positioned to anchor the design before filling in with honesty and Iris foetidissima *seeds*

Pick the flowers on a dry day, when the bloom is at its best. Cut the stems to about 4 cm (1½ in) long. Put 5 cm (2 in) of the desiccant in an airtight tin or box and place the blossoms on top of this, so they do not touch one another. Shake the desiccant on top, making sure it goes between all the petals. Then cover the flowers completely. Replace the lid tightly, making sure the container is airtight.

Flowers can take anything from a few days to several weeks to dry out, according to the type of flower and the type of desiccant. Silica gel is the most rapid. Borax used on its own can take some time. When dry, the petals should be really crisp. If they are not, return them to the desiccant for a few days.

Remove them from the container when they are ready and gently shake off the desiccant. Brush the

The piece of bark that provides the focal point here was positioned first. The dried oats were put down next, after which the outline was completed and the design filled in. White-faced hardboard, against which the shades of brown are extremely effective, was used for the background

---

petals with a small paint brush and remove loose grains, but do handle carefully since they will be very fragile and brittle. If you want to give the petals a sheen you can paint them carefully with oil. Any loose petals, or those that have fallen off completely, can be glued back on again. If you want to use the blooms in an arrangement, it will probably be necessary to give them false stems.

Suitable flowers include buttercups, violets, pansies, anemones, daisies, primroses, polyanthus,

asters, single roses, sweet peas and lilies-of-the-valley.

Some ways of using preserved material

Plant materials, particularly leaves that go limp when preserved, can be made firm by wiring. Leaves are easily wired. Use a stub wire, of medium thickness, obtainable from florists. Cut the wire about 2·5 cm (1 in) longer than the leaf and tape it with a clear sticky tape to the centre of the leaf, leaving the excess protruding from the bottom of the leaf. This can then be stuck into a false stem (such as those taken and

---

Tiny pictures can be just as attractive as large ones, although often they are rather more fiddly to make. Here a tiny triangular design of daisies was built up on a background of green Dralon

dried from *Staychs lanata* honesty, stems that do not have a hollow interior) if you want to make the leaf a certain height for an arrangement.

Sprays of leaves that are limp can be wired individually and the whole spray can be given a longer stem by hooking the wire round the point where the lowest branch joins the stem and twisting the two ends together. These can be pushed and glued into a false stem, using either a natural stalk, as above, or a length of thin stick.

Some flowerheads will need to be given false stems if they are wanted for arrangements since the natural stems do not dry satisfactorily. Helichrysum is a good example of this.

To give helichrysum a false stem, pick with a 1-cm (½-in) stalk left on the flower. As soon as you have picked the flowers, cut off a piece of stub wire about 4 cm (1½ in) long. Push it into the flowerhead from the back. Leave it there as the flower dries. It will rust in place and be impossible to get out. When the flower is dry, you can push the protruding piece of wire into any length of false stem you require.

You can push the wire through the dried flower by making a hook in the wire and gently pulling it

Some raw materials—feather and cone

through the centre of the flower-head. But the flower is a little more fragile to handle at this stage and since the wire will not then rust into place, it will not be as firm.

Fir cones

All types of fir cones are useful in arrangements of preserved plant material. They can be used on their own or as a basis for making flowers.

If you want to give a cone a false stem so that it can stand in an arrangement, cut off two lengths of stub wire. Slip these into either side of the cone, as close to the bottom as possible. This will help to make the stem stand vertically. Twist the wires together at either side of the cone and pull them down to the bottom. Twist them together in the centre of the base and push both ends into a false stem.

If the cone is a long, thin type, one length of wire can be used, twisted round the cone, and the end stuck into a false stem in the same way.

Do not be too worried if you feel the wiring is very obvious or prominent. It will generally be hidden by other material in an arrangement.

Cones are also very useful for making your own dried flowers.

Wood shavings make lovely, natural-looking petals for these flowers. Cut the petals any shape you like and either slot them into the fir cones, or if that does not seem very secure, glue them in place. You can produce an endless variety of flowers in this way, either using whole cones, cutting them in half or just using a small piece from the bottom. Alternatively, you can use the bottom piece of a large cone to form the petals and stick a small flower, such as a helichrysum bloom, in the hollowed-out centre.

Wood shavings can be used to make petals for other flowers, too. For example, you can wire a helichrysum flower and then stick wood shaving petals around it. Depending on how the wood has been cut, you can sometimes damp the petals and roll them up, securing them with an elastic band until they dry, when the petals will be prettily curled. You can also dye the wood shavings, either with a commercial dye if you want a particular shade, or by boiling them with bruised beetroot (for red), or with turmeric (for yellow).

(Left) Plant material used in this picture could be grown in a small garden. The centre was found and the globe artichoke secured in position first. Being large and also delicate, it needed a firm base to keep it securely in position. The beech leaves were positioned next, to establish the perimeter of the design. After that the material was positioned from the outside and brought in towards the centre. In a design such as this, working in this way ensures that each piece of material is correctly positioned in relation to the other pieces of the design

(Right) In this picture, although the central point was established first, the central feature was actually the last to be secured in the design. This enabled it to stand out from the rest of the picture

*Detail of a framed collage made up
of seedheads and fir cones*

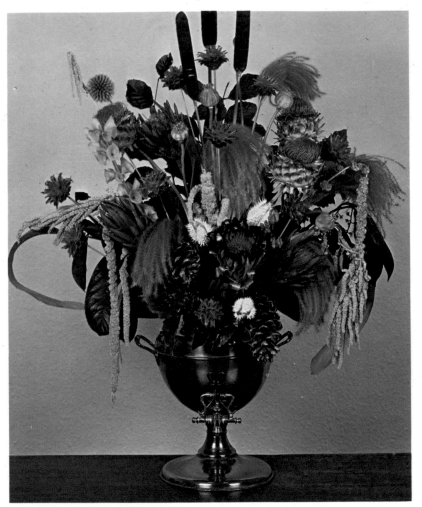

Arrangements from preserved material

Any arrangement you make from preserved plant material will depend upon two main factors: the material you have available and where you intend it to go.

If the arrangement is for a dining table, then remember it has to be viewed from all sides, but it must not be too high or too obtrusive. In this instance, if you are doing a circular or oval arrangement, start by positioning material at the north, south, east and west points and then build up the design into a low cushion shape. If it is wanted for a corner spot, then concentrate on the front aspect, but fill in the back since it will still be viewed from the sides and you do not want these to

118

Urn arrangement (1)

look bare. If you want an arrangement to stand on a shelf above a radiator, then do not fill in the back. This will enable you to push the arrangement right back to the wall, which means it will be less affected by the heat. Laurel leaves are less affected by heat and last longer than beech leaves put in this position. Avoid any foliage drooping down in front of the radiator, as the heat will be too intense and will soon spoil it.

Decide on the height and basic shape of the arrangement and position the pieces you have chosen to achieve this effect. Begin with height. Fill in with the remaining material. Obviously the colour scheme will depend both on the

colours you have available and the room's predominant colour, but keep the darker and more dramatic material towards the base of the arrangement so that it does not become top heavy.

An arrangement of preserved material tends to be more static than that of fresh flowers, so it should be made interesting as well as decorative. One way of providing interest is by using an unusual container, which becomes part of the decoration. If you use a basket or a teapot, for example, put the high material behind the handle and the low material in front, so you can see the handle and pick up the arrangement by it. Cross-cuts of wood or branches make interesting bases, too. Let them dry out slowly and leave them natural or darken them by rubbing with linseed oil. You can varnish them if you want them to look shiny. A branch from a silver birch cut into a short length makes an interesting base, but you will have to saw one side flat to stop it from rolling about.

Unlikely though it may seem, old tin cans—sardines, herring, pet food—make very good containers. Cover them with material or paint them to blend with your arrangement.

Preserved plant material can be supported by plasticine, dry plastic foam, pinholders or even a plaster-of-paris base. Of these, dry plastic foam is probably the most satisfactory and is available in oblong, round or square blocks from most florists. Cut it with a knife to whatever size and shape you want. It can be held in place with an oasis holder (a small plastic object consisting of four sharp prongs) and some oasis fix. Both are obtainable from most florists.

Push a little oasis fix on to the base of the container and push the oasis holder on to it. Then push the plastic foam on to the prongs, which will hold it quite firmly. Alternatively, you can push the foam directly on to a pin holder, in which case cover the pin holder with a piece of nylon cut from a pair of tights first. This greatly facilitates the removal of the foam later.

Urn arrangement (1)

An arrangement of this nature should be done in the place where it is to stand.

1 In this instance, a pin holder with dry foam pushed on to it was put into a plastic bowl and then into the copper container. This was done to form a heavy base to the arrangement.

2 The height of the arrangement was first determined by placing the three bullrushes at the back.

3 The width and shape of the sides was set by the placing of the laurels and beech.

4 The artichoke heads were placed next since they were among the largest of the material to be used in the arrangement. It was therefore important to position them early on and then to work around them.

5 Fir cones and protea were placed at the bottom of the arrangement to balance the artichoke heads.

6 The central areas of the design were filled in with the smaller items of material, such as the poppy and thistle heads and the bells of Ireland.

7 Finally, the more flowing shapes such as the aspidistra leaves were positioned to give the arrangement some downward movement.

Driftwood arrangement (2)

An interestingly shaped or attractively marked or coloured piece of wood picked up on a country walk, or some driftwood from the beach, can be used as an integral part of a preserved plant arrangement. Here, the important thing to remember is not to obscure the piece of wood but to arrange your material around it so as to show it off to the best advantage.

Scrub the wood with a mild detergent solution and then let it dry in the sunlight or indoors in a warm, dry place. Remove or prune

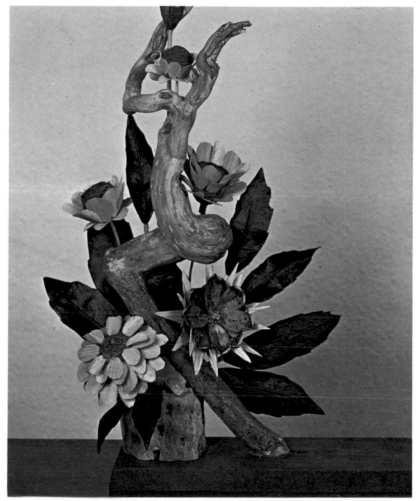

away any bits you do not want. Sandpaper it if you want it to have a really smooth appearance, but remember that this takes away the natural texture. You can then either leave it natural, wax it if you want a mild shine, varnish it if you want a more pronounced shine, or paint, stain or blacken it by burning if you want to produce some special effect.

1 In this arrangement, the driftwood was left natural and mounted on a block of wood. This was done by drilling a hole in the wood and gluing the driftwood to it. You may also find it necessary to screw the piece of wood in to make sure it is sufficiently firm.

2 Secure the dry foam, to take the preserved material, to the base behind the piece of wood, using a

Driftwood arrangement (2)

pin holder, or an oasis fix.

3 Dried acuba leaves, wired and mounted on sticks were positioned first.

4 The cone and wood shaving flowers were then positioned. Note how few pieces are used in the arrangement and how the wood shaving petals complement the colour of the driftwood.

Small arrangement for a radiator shelf (3)

This design was planned to be triangular rather than symmetrical. Oasis fix was positioned on the log to secure the holder and the plastic foam.

The design was achieved by following the usual principles. The

119

highest point was fixed first by positioning the tallest material. The sloping outline of the right-hand side was done next and then the left-hand side, taking care to keep this in a vertical line. Finally, the inside of the design was worked.

Brown and cream arrangement (4)

This design was planned using only natural-coloured material. The second base was chipboard, covered with a neutrally coloured matting. Suitable for a corner in a room of almost any colour scheme, the design was built up on the usual lines by establishing the height and the shape of the sides, before filling in the middle of the design.

Rabbit's ears arrangement (5)

A pinholder was used in the base of this arrangement to give it bottom weight. The container was a tin covered with pink Dralon and mounted on a board covered in the same material to highlight the colour of the arrangement.

Figurine arrangement (6)

The interest in this arrangement is obviously provided by the figurine container. The design was planned to follow the sweep of the figure's left hand. The height of the design was first established, using the long grasses. These should be roughly one and a half times the height of the container. The right-hand side was also worked with grasses following the form of the figure. Then the left side was worked to give the arrangement balance. Finally, the dried blue and white larkspur flowers were positioned.

Grasses in oval hanger (7)

This arrangement of dried grasses was done in a small round bowl, although the arrangement itself was oval. The oval outline was established by positioning the longer grasses and rushes and the design

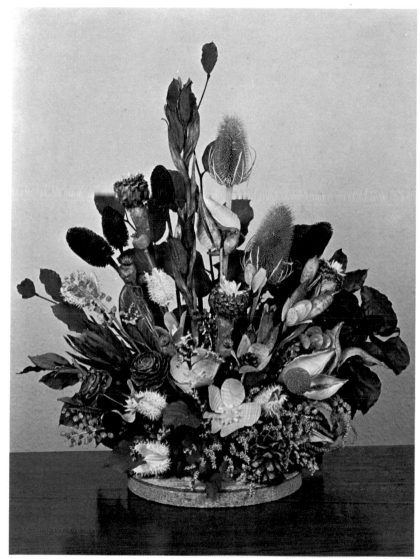

Brown and cream arrangement (4)

was then worked in towards the centre, using other types of grasses.

Candelabra arrangement (8)

The two balancing arrangements were placed in the outer holders of a table candelabra to form a pleasant conversation piece. The composition is made up of grasses with grape hyacinth seedheads added, together with pressed sprays of fir tree, dried *Helleborus*, and *Acroclinium*. The candle completes the effect, but it should be able to burn safely.

Radiator arrangement (9)

The base used is a small silver birch log into which a selection of natural

and coloured grasses has been set. Fir cones, flowers and seedheads have been added and the arrangement lightened by the insertion of bought bleached ferns.

Corner arrangement (10)

This pretty little arrangement in a silver birch log base may be used for a corner arrangement or placed on a table or against a wall. It is composed of mauve straw flowers, white helichrysum, *Acroclinium*, honestry, white statice, bougainvillaea bracts and a selection of grasses.

Small arrangement for radiator shelf (3)

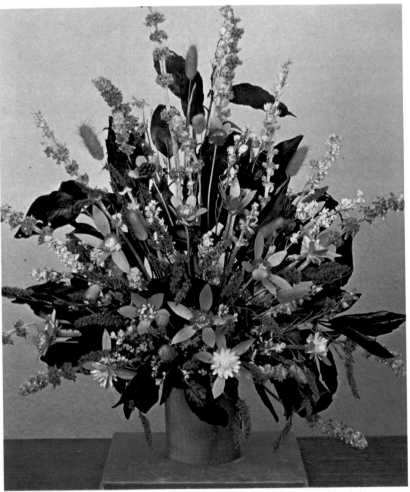

Pictures from preserved plant material

Pictures made from dried and glycerined leaves, flowers and seedheads differ from a collage in that they use only natural material. For this reason it is important to keep all the material as natural-looking as possible. You will find you will tire of them less quickly and this is an important consideration since they last a very long time.

Decide first on the colour scheme of your picture. This will generally be determined, as with an arrangement, by the place in which it is to hang. Do not mix colours too much in a picture; instead, combine different shades and tones around one basic colour. The colours must also harmonize with the back-

Rabbit's ears arrangement (5)

ground. For example, shades of pink or orange flowers display well against a brown background.

Every picture should have a focal point to act as an anchor for the design. This is the first thing to decide upon and also to fix. It may be at any point in the picture, the centre or to one side, but in a symmetrical design, it should be positioned in the bottom centre of the picture. Incidentally, if you have decided the focal point of the picture is to be in the centre, measure this point from the sides and top to make sure you really do find the centre. Use the most dramatic material of your picture for the focal point— either a large seedhead or flower or, perhaps, a piece of bark or a shell. If you use a flower, it should be the

biggest and darkest one you have.

The next step is to establish the basic outline of the picture. Depending a little on the design, this is generally best done with leaves, which tend to be larger and more uniformly and symmetrically shaped. Sprays of leaves, such as glycerined peonies, for example, can be most useful for giving you an interesting outline.

Finally, fill in the design with the remainder of the material you have planned to use, flowers, seedheads and grasses. At this point, do not worry about making the design too symmetrical and be guided by the shapes, making them work for you rather than trying to mould them into the way you think they should look. The balance of the design is obviously very important in pictures. In general, keep the lighter-coloured material around the outside and put the stronger-coloured, darker material in the centre so that your eye is more readily drawn to this point. Do not overcrowd a picture by putting in too much. A good rule to follow is 'if in doubt, leave out'.

Affix material to the background with clear glue, which should always be used very sparingly. It is much easier to add more than to try to get rid of any excess. This is particularly important if your background material is velvet. It is impossible to remove excess glue from velvet. It will show and spoil the whole picture. When sticking down leaves, squeeze a small amount down the centre rib of the leaf and then put a few dots here and there towards the outside edges. Do not force a leaf or spray to lie absolutely flat on the background. A slight three-dimensional effect is more interesting and attractive.

As well as the natural material, you will need a flat base. The best material to use for this is plywood, which is thick enough not to bend and warp and is easily cut to any size. You can stain it, paint it with emulsion paint, cover it with any sort of fabric, polish it or leave it plain. Hardboard is also satisfactory and may be painted or left natural. Offcuts are perfectly adequate and are often available quite cheaply from do-it-yourself stores. White-faced hardboard is useful if you want a plain white background to your picture, and although the surface is shiny, you will find the glue still adheres to it quite firmly.

If you intend to cover the background with such fabric as hessian, furnishing velvet or any thick material, you can use a strong cardboard. Make sure you glue the fabric down really firmly, stretching it to get a smooth, wrinkle-free surface. Provided the fabric is thick, the glue will not seep or show through, but if there is any doubt, cut the fabric larger than the background and glue it down on the back.

Keep a look out at jumble sales or secondhand shops for old picture frames. If they are slightly damaged you can often repair them with a touch of paint. An old gilt frame that is chipped can be repaired with a plastic filler and then regilded with gold paint. A little make-do-and-mend can work wonders.

Have scissors and tweezers handy as you do your picture. You will find you need them constantly to trim bits off stalks, remove the odd leaf and so on. Tweezers can help you to position small bits of material that may be too fiddly to handle with your fingers.

Velcro is very useful for hanging your picture and it does far less damage to the wall than nails or picture hooks. However, it is only effective on frames that are flat-backed and not too heavy. You will only need a piece of Velcro about 2·5 cm (1 in) long. Stick one piece of this to the centre of the back of the picture and the other piece to the wall at the point where you wish the picture to hang. Leave both pieces to dry before pressing

Figurine arrangement (6)

Grasses in oval hanger (7)

the picture to the wall. If the frame is very heavy, put small hooks in it.

Pressing flowers

The main difference between pressed flowers and leaves and plant material preserved by other methods is that pressing results in a completely flat finish, whereas the other methods retain a three-dimensional effect. Pressed material is ideal for making pictures or greetings cards, for decorating the sides of a lampshade, a waste-paper basket or a plain china pot, for sticking on to a bookmark or under a transparent finger plate for a door. However they are used, it is important to cover them either with glass, in the case of a picture, or with

transparent adhesive paper so as to exclude all air. They will reabsorb moisture if exposed to the air, particularly if humid.

Pressing reduces or eliminates the water content of the plant, so that it will not shrivel in its preserved state. Most flowers and leaves can be pressed, although the flatter, simply constructed types are generally more successful than those that have many fleshy petals or very thick, hard centres. Flowers with these characteristics can be pressed, if you so wish, but they need extra care and different treatment from the others.

The point at which flowers are gathered for pressing is critical. Clearly they should be at their best,

A selection of pressed flower pictures, kindly lent by Evelyn Rodwell-Jones

for they will certainly not improve or change miraculously during the pressing process. Choose a dry, sunny day and pick after the dew has gone in the morning, or before the petals begin to close up in the evening. Flowers must be quite dry before pressing or they will be spoiled by unsightly spots or by patches of mould or mildew.

Material should be as fresh as possible for pressing. You should press it as soon as you can after picking. If you find you cannot press the material straight away, for some reason or another, put the

124

items carefully into polythene bags or plastic boxes or stand them in water. This will help to keep them fresh a little longer, provided you have not crushed or damaged them.

Equipment for pressing flowers

Little in the way of sophisticated equipment is needed for pressing flowers. Indeed, at its simplest all you need is a supply of blotting paper and some thick, heavy books, preferably with matt pages as they produce better results. Large leaves can be placed between sheets of newspaper or blotting paper and placed under a carpet or heavy rug that is in constant use, provided the rug does not wrinkle or move.

Many shops sell special flower presses which consist of sheets of corrugated paper held between two squares of plywood. A screw and wing nut joins the plywood squares at each corner and each unit can be tightened to exert pressure.

Preparation for pressing arrangement

Check the flowers before you press them to make sure no flies or insects are lodged inside or between the petals. Cut pieces of blotting paper to fit the pages of the book or the cardboard squares of the flower press. Place the flowers face down on to one of these pieces, flattening the heads and evenly spreading out the petals.

Space out the flowers so that there is plenty of room between them. They should not touch one another.

Flowers such as daffodils can either be dismantled and each part pressed separately for reassembling later according to how you want to use them, or they can be cut in half longitudinally and each piece pressed. Hard centred flowers such as rubeckia daisies are best dismantled altogether and the petals individually pressed. The centres

do not look attractive when pressed and it is much better to give them a false centre from another flower when you come to reassemble them.

In many instances you will get better results if you press the flower stalks separately from their flowerheads. But not always. When pressing flowers and stalks together, coax the stalks into gentle curves rather than preserving them in straight lines. These, you will find, rarely fit sympathetically into a design or picture. It is also a good idea to press a few extra petals. Then, should any petals become damaged in the pressing, you will have some reserves to fall back on.

Pressing flowers

Arrange your flowers on blotting paper, cover them with another sheet and sandwich them either between the matt pages of the book, or between the cardboard leaves of the flower press. Put more books or bricks on top, or tighten up the screws on the press. If you are pressing several sandwiches of flowers at one time it is a good idea to label them with tags protruding from the pages or press, giving the name of the flowers or leaves and the date of pressing.

Different types of flowers and leaves take varying amounts of time to press satisfactorily. The very least amount of time is four to six weeks and, ideally, you should not disturb the material during this time. If, however, you are pressing very fleshy flowers, you could check to see if the top piece of blotting paper has become saturated and if it has, replace it with another piece.

The longer you leave the flowers to press, the more papery thin they become and the better the colours will be preserved. Many experts recommend leaving them in their presses for a full year. Do bear in mind that the colours of pressed flowers will fade when exposed to light over a period of time. Blues and violet colours, in particular, often fade to cream.

Pressed flowers will also reabsorb moisture over a period of time, at which point they will go mouldy. Store them in a dry box, kept in a cool place until you want them.

Keep your pressed flowers and leaves either between sheets of blotting paper in a warm, dry flat place, or in clearly marked envelopes. Do not mix different species together. Keeping them separate enables you to make an instant assessment of your material to plan your designs accordingly.

A pressed leaf picture

Pressed flower pictures

The material you have available will largely determine the pattern and the design of your picture. Having gathered the material, decide on the sort of background it needs. Strong paper or artist's board makes the best background for pictures. This is available in a variety of colours and shades. Select a colour that will show the flowers off to their best advantage. Remember, the materials should dominate, not the background colour.

Cut the background to the size of the frame. Any sort of frame may be used for your picture, either modern or traditional, but must have a glass front that completely excludes air. When they are exposed to air they soon deteriorate.

Having cut your background material to size and selected the flowers, leaves and stalks you wish to use, decide on the basic shape and outline of your picture. It may be a symmetrical design radiating out from a central focal point, or it may be a sweeping crescent shape. If it is a symmetrical design, remember you must select flowerheads and leaves that match in size and colour.

Work on a flat surface, out of all draughts. These can cause havoc with your design. Position all items of material to complete the whole design before fixing anything in place. Begin by placing the main flowers or leaves of the design, remembering these may well be flowers such as roses, which will need reassembling. Fill in with the leaves and flower stalks, shifting them around with the end of a fine paint brush until you are satisfied with their position.

You must constantly bear in mind the overall shape and balance of the picture and the relationship of the flowers and leaves as you work. Do not overcrowd the design or it will look cramped and unattractive.

Only when you are quite satisfied with the arrangement, fix it in place. Use clear glue very sparingly and apply it to the backs of stalks, flowerheads, petals and leaves with a cocktail stick, or matchstick, or with the pointed end of a paintbrush. There is no need to apply glue all over the petals or the leaves, just a few spots here and there are quite sufficient. Leave the rest of the design in place as you glue each piece down.

Press the glass of the frame down on to the picture as soon as you have finished gluing the design. Try to make sure there are no bulky pieces of material which would prevent the flatter area from coming into contact with the glass.

Avoid hanging the picture in a position exposed to very strong sunlight which would fade the colours of the flowers. Pressed flowers tend to fade over a period of time, and this is a factor you should bear in mind as you plan your designs and mix your colours. Yellow and orange flowers tend to retain their colour quite well although some will eventually fade to cream. Larkspur and delphinium will keep their blueness far longer then many other flowers.

Candelabra (8)

Greetings cards

Beautiful, personalized greetings cards can be created for your friends from preserved flowers, designed to suit all occasions.

Apply the same principles to making cards, as to creating pictures. First, cut your card to the size you want. Then select the material and position the whole design on the card. When you are satisfied with it, glue it very carefully in to place. Cover the whole card with transparent adhesive film. This needs very careful handling to ensure that it is really flat with no air bubbles trapped underneath it. Press it down firmly round the edges of the card and then trim off any surplus.

Door finger plates

Pressed flowers can be used to make attractive finger plates to fix on to a plain door. You can do this either by planning and fixing a design on to a piece of card and then gluing this to the back of the plate, or the design can be put straight on to the back of a transparent plate, so that it is the door that creates the background.

Hints

Do not treat leaves too early, while they are soft and immature.

Do not delay picking until the leaves are beginning to turn colour.

Do not allow stems to dry out during the preserving process—a transparent jar makes it easier to see the level of the solution.

Do not be afraid to wash preserved leaves which have become dusty and dirty in warm soapy water. Be sure they are quite dry again before storing.

Do experiment with different plants; it costs little and can be a very worthwhile investment which provides interesting material for use during the winter months.

Shelf arrangement (9)

Corner arrangement (10)

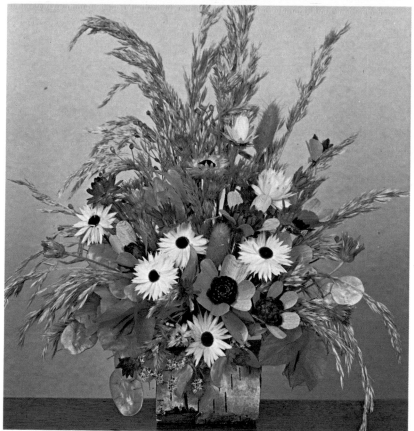

Books for further reference

Complete Book of Flower Preservation	G. Condon	Hale	1974
Collingridge Book of Dried and Pressed Flowers	Jane Derbyshire R. Burgess	Hamlyn	1975
Pressed Flower Pictures: a Victorian Art Revisited	Pamela McDowall	Lutterworth	1969
Drying and Preserving Flowers	Winefrede Morrison	Batsford	1973
Flowers for Pleasure: Craft and Decorative Ideas	Nicol Kit	Lutterworth	1974
Art and Science of Flowers	Nicolette Scourse	Michael Joseph	1973
Flower Arrangement from Wild Plants	Violet Stevenson	Dent	1972
Creative Flower Arrangement	Jean Taylor	Stanley Paul	1973
Flower Arranging	Jean Taylor	Macdonald Educational	1978
Art of Dried and Pressed Flowers	Pamela Westland Paula Gritchley	Ward Lock	1974

Conversion Tables

All weights and measures in this book are given in the metric system, followed by the imperial in brackets. Conversions are correctly adjusted within one system and have been taken up or down to round figures in all instances to make for ease of working. Do not worry if you find that the conversions given differ slightly from those given in the table below, which is for general reference. Providing you follow one set of measures—either the imperial or the metric—these variations are of no importance. Do not attempt to mix the measurements, or the amounts will not be correctly adjusted.

Solid Measures

Metric	Imperial
25 g	1 oz
50 g	2 oz
75 g	3 oz
100-125 g	4 oz
225 g	8 oz
450 g	1 lb
900 g	2 lb
1 kg	2 lb 3 oz
1·1 kg	2 lb 8 oz
1·4 kg	3 lb
1·6 kg	3 lb 8 oz
1·8 kg	4 lb
2 kg	4 lb 8 oz

Liquid Measures

Metric	Imperial
25 ml	1 fl oz
50 ml	2 fl oz
75 ml	3 fl oz
100 ml	4 fl oz
275 ml	$\frac{1}{2}$ pint
575 ml	1 pint
1 litre	$1\frac{3}{4}$ pint

Linear Measures

Metric	Imperial
2·5 cm	1 in
5 cm	2 in
7·5 cm	3 in
10 cm	4 in
12·5 cm	5 in
15 cm	6 in
30·5 cm	1 ft
91·5 cm	1 yd
1 m	1·093 yd

Glossary

amulet a charm against evil (corn dollies)

Ankh ancient Egyptian symbol of eternal life (corn dollies)

base stake one of the strong rods on which the base of a basket is woven

base weaver the material used to weave the base of a basket

basket willow *Salix triandra*, the willow used in basketry

bodkin a sharp spike used to pierce rods or open up spaces (basketry)

bolt unit of measurement in basketry: a bundle of willow or rush equivalent to the quantity of fresh material around which a man's arms will reach

to border to turn down the side stakes decoratively, so preventing the edge of the basket fraying

boss an ornamental circle (corn dollies)

bought willow commercial willow sold by wholesalers and craft shops (basketry)

brown willow commercial willow dried in its bark (basketry)

buff willow commercial willow peeled after boiling; this process stains the wood the colour of pale cocoa (basketry)

butt the end of a rod originally attached to the plant; the thick end of a rod (basketry)

butterfly butterfly-shaped implement used to carry the weft across the warp (weaving)

bystake a second stake placed beside a side stake to strengthen it (basketry)

cane centre cane; lengths of creeper pith processed to various thicknesses (basketry)

to card to tease or comb out fleece with a pair of implements called carders (spinning)

carder an implement with metal spikes, used in pairs to tease out matted or dirty pieces of fleece before spinning (see spinning figure 3)

cavity wheat hollow wheat (corn dollies)

chain pair alternate rows of pair and reverse pair (basketry)

chain wale alternate rows of wale and reverse wale (basketry)

cochineal a dye made from the beetle *Coccus cactii* (dyeing)

coloured straws short pieces of straw, dyed in various colours (corn dollies)

to contract to place the working straw inside the straw of the preceding round (corn dollies)

corn dolly a general term applied to objects made of tied and plaited straw at harvest time

corn mother a name given in Scotland to a straw figure dressed as an old woman

cornucopia horn of plenty, represented in art as overflowing with flowers, fruit and corn (corn dollies)

crosspiece the horizontal arm of a cross (corn dollies)

desiccant an agent for the extraction of water from plant material (flowercraft)

English rand weaving with as many rods as there are stakes put in one at a time (basketry)

to expand to place the working straw outside the straw of the preceding round

false bottom a rim of weaving that helps a round-bottomed basket to stand well (basketry)

fitch a decorative space in weaving (basketry)

folded plait a plait that is folded as opposed to bent over (corn dollies)

follow-on pushing the ends of a three-rod border back to the wrong side to fill in any gaps (basketry)

French rand a technique in which as many rods as stakes are woven simultaneously (basketry)

French wale a technique in which the sides of a basket are woven with a particular type of waling (basketry)

glycerine mix one part glycerine to two parts boiling water, used for preserving plant material (flowercraft)

group-linked plait a plait formed by dividing straws into equal groups that are linked by a travelling straw (corn dollies)

handle bow a strong rod used to form a basket handle

handle winder a very thin rod used to cover the main handle rod of a basket

harvest cross a design in straw in the form of a cross (corn dollies)

harvest festival a church thanksgiving service after gathering in the crops (corn dollies)

harvest home a celebration at the close of harvesting (corn dollies)

harvest maid one of the many names used to describe the straw dollies made at harvest time

harvest supper a feast to celebrate the completion of harvest (corn dollies)

headless straws straw from which the head has been removed (corn dollies)

lazy kate a simple holder to take the winding bobbin when spinning

liner a thick rod put in the sides of a basket as they are being woven to make a space into which the handle bow can be inserted (basketry)

Lord Horkey a man elected by his fellow farm workers to collect money for drinks at the completion of harvest (corn dollies)

medallion single straws wound and joined round a cross from the centre outwards (corn

to mellow	dollies) to wrap wet rods up after soaking in order to complete the internal dampening process, at the same time draining off the outside (basketry)	**scaffold knot**	dollies) a knot used to tie a horizontal bar to a perpendicular bar, as in scaffolding (weaving)
mock French	imitating French rand with two fewer weavers (basketry)	**seedhead**	the seed case left on the stalk after the petals have fallen (flowercraft)
mock wale	starting a band of French rand by going in front of two stakes instead of one (basketry)	**shed** **shed stick**	an opening made between the warps for the passage of the weft (weaving) a length of wood inserted between a certain arrangement of warps to keep them apart to enable the weft to pass across the frame (weaving)
mould	a hard form used to shape a soft basket		
neck	a sheaf of corn; also the name of a certain type of corn dolly		
niddy noddy	a gadget used to hank wool after spinning	**side weaver**	material used to weave the side of a basket
nodes	the joints in a straw stalk (corn dollies)	**to slew**	to rand with two or more rods used as one (basketry)
nut	*Corylus avellana*, hazel (basketry)	**to slype**	to sharpen the end of a rod, usually to a very long point so it will easily fit into a gap in the weaving (basketry)
oasis	a trade name for plastic foam used by flower-arrangers, but generally applied to any brand (flowercraft)		
oasis fix	a very sticky green substance used to fix oasis holders on to a log, piece of tin or wood, or any other base (flowercraft)	**spiral**	straws plaited to form a conical or cylindrical shape (corn dollies)
		spiral plait	straws plaited to form a conical or cylindrical shape, with or without core (corn dollies)
oasis holder	a gadget used to hold plastic foam in flower arrangements; the foam is pressed down on to the holder's upward-pointing, wide-set prongs (flowercraft)	**stake**	material that forms the skeleton of a basket
		to step-up	to make complete rows of waling instead of a spiral (basketry)
osier	basket-maker's willow, usually variety *Salix triandra* (basketry)	**template**	a metal guide for cutting patterns (corn dollies)
pairing	a line of pair weave (basketry)	**threader**	a tool for threading rushes into the weaving of a basket; it is usually a sacking needle set in a handle (basketry)
to pair	to weave with two rods at once (basketry)		
Palembang	an Asian creeper, much stiffer than centre cane, with its bark still attached (basketry)	**three-rod**	a type of border in which the rods twist round each other (basketry)
peeled stake	a stake with the bark removed (basketry)	**tip**	the growing end of a twig (basketry)
peg	a short twig pushed into the handle bow below the border of a basket to prevent it being pulled out (basketry)	**trac**	a type of border in which each rod follows the previous one (basketry)
		trefoil	three-lobed ornamentation (corn dollies)
		triangular plait	four straws worked in spiral plait round a core of a single straw with a wire inserted (corn dollies)
pinholder	a gadget used to hold heavy material in flower arrangements; the type that holds water looks well on its own without a vase or other container (flowercraft)		
		to trim	to cut off all protruding ends (basketry); to cut to an even length (corn dollies)
to prick	to push the bodkin through a rod so that it will bend easily (basketry)	**Turkey knotting**	a type of weave (see weaving figure 22)
raffia	a kind of palm; fibres from its leaves are used to tie up plants (flowercraft)	**Tyrolean plait**	a flat, folded plait from Austria (corn dollies)
to rand	to weave with one rod (basketry)	**to upset**	to turn the side stakes up after inserting them into the base of a basket
rand stroke	one movement of one rod in a weave; a step (basketry)	**vertical wheel**	a spinning wheel which has the spinning unit mounted above the driving wheel
rod	a single twig of one year's growth (basketry)	**to wale**	to weave with three or more rods at once (basketry)
rope plait	a plait made of straw or rush using a twisting technique; it is used for decorative and domestic purposes (corn dollies)	**waler**	a rod used in waling (basketry)
rush	*Scirpus lacustris*, Coopers' rush (basketry); marsh or waterside plant (corn	**warp**	the threads that run lengthwise in the frame; the weft threads cross the warp threads to form the web (weaving)

warping pole an additional length of wood used to take an extended warp in certain weaving frames (see Salish frame, weaving figure 24)

wattle familiar name for hazel (basketry); fleshy appendage under throat of cock (corn dollies)

wattle and daub woven hazel hurdles covered with plaster (basketry)

weaver any rod that weaves in and out of stakes (basketry)

weaving hook an implement, invented by the author of *Spinning, Dyeing and Weaving*, that takes the weft across the warp (see weaving figure 15)

weft the threads that cross the frame interlacing the warp threads at right angles (weaving); yarn to be used for weft threads (weaving); strips of cane, palm leaf, used as the filling in weaving baskets (basketry)

weld *Reseda luteola*, a plant which yields a yellow dye; the dye obtained from this plant (dyeing)

whorl a small fly wheel attached to the spindle of a spinning wheel to maintain or regulate the speed (spinning); a set of leaves, flowers, parts of the flower springing from the stem at the same level and encircling it (flowercraft)

wicker a pliant twig or small rod, usually of willow, used for making baskets; an osier (basketry)

willow narrow-leaved plants of the *Salix* family

wired filling a filling of dried flowers secured with wire (corn dollies)

withy familiar name for willow (basketry)

woad *Isatis tinctoria*, a plant formerly used for blue dye, called dyeing woad or garden woad; a blue dye prepared from the leaves, which are powdered and fermented; wild woad is the popular name for *Reseda luteola* (see weld)

wood stretcher a piece of wood, cut to size, for preserving the shape of a corn dolly while it is drying out

Index